Natasha Khalique is an award-winning specialist family law barrister at Exchange Chambers and a door tenant at 1GC Family Law. She practises exclusively in financial remedy, international, public and private children law, with distinctive expertise in the validity of marriages involving the Islamic *Nikah*. Alongside this, she has developed a leading and fast-growing niche in neurodivergence within family law. As an AuDHD practitioner, Natasha draws on her lived experience to advocate effectively for neurodivergent clients and is increasingly regarded as the go-to barrister in this field, regularly instructed in complex cases across England and Wales. She also serves on the FLANC Advisory Committee.

Natasha's professional excellence has been recognised through multiple accolades. She won Legal Professional of the Year (2023) at the JCI Manchester Awards. In 2024, she received the National Resolution Rising Star Award, which celebrates emerging talent and recognises practitioners who have demonstrated exceptional promise as future leaders of family justice. The judges praised her as "a champion for neurodiversity in the legal profession." She was also shortlisted for Barrister/KC of the Year at the Manchester Legal Awards 2025 and Community Champion at the Manchester Resolution Awards. Natasha is ranked Tier 2 in *The Legal 500* for Divorce and Finance proceedings.

# A Practical Guide to Neurodivergence in Family Law

# A Practical Guide to Neurodivergence in Family Law

Natasha Khalique

Law Brief Publishing

Published 2026 by Law Brief Publishing, an imprint of Law Brief Publishing Ltd
30 The Parks
Minehead
Somerset
TA24 8BT

www.lawbriefpublishing.com

Paperback: 978-1-918241-11-2

*If the fifteen-year-old Natasha had been told she would one day write a book about ADHD and neurodivergence, she would never have believed it. My heartfelt thanks to everyone who has supported me along the way, to my family for their unwavering encouragement, and to God for guiding me through every stage of this journey. I would not change a thing.*

*For the neurodivergent individuals whose experiences are so often overlooked or misinterpreted: may this book help ensure you are seen more clearly, understood with greater care, and contribute in some small way to breaking down the barriers you face.*

# PREFACE

The idea for this book emerged from both professional experience and personal reflection. As a neurodivergent barrister with autism and ADHD, I have often noticed that understanding of neurodivergent conditions within the family justice system varies widely. Many practitioners work with great care and intention yet may not have had access to the information or guidance needed to recognise how neurodivergence can influence communication, behaviour or sensory processing. Without that context, misunderstandings can arise, sometimes shaping the way a case is approached or interpreted, even when everyone involved is aiming for the best possible outcome.

I have also spent time considering how these situations might feel if the roles were reversed. What if I were not the barrister, but the parent sitting anxiously in conference, processing information differently or expressing myself in ways that did not fit expected patterns? It highlighted for me how important it is that representatives and decision makers understand neurodivergence not as a trend or passing topic of interest, but as a lifelong way of experiencing the world. These reflections reinforced the need for clearer guidance and practical tools to support both practitioners and the individuals they work with, particularly in matters involving significant decisions about children and family life.

This book is my attempt to bridge that gap. It brings together in one practical place the core knowledge, legal frameworks and day to day tools that I wish every practitioner had when working with neurodivergent clients. The opening chapters share my own journey, not for sentimentality, but to illustrate how neurodivergence can manifest from childhood through adolescence and adulthood and to shed light on the real-world barriers and misunderstandings that many neurodivergent people encounter. Later chapters explore the meaning and scope of neurodivergence, with focused discussions on ADHD and autism, before turning to intersectionality, duties within the legal framework, barriers to participation and the realities of representing neurodivergent individuals in both public law and private law contexts.

My hope is that this guide supports practitioners in recognising when neurodivergence may be a key factor in a case, understanding how it might present and adapting their approach in a way that promotes fairness and meaningful participation. If sharing my experiences encourages even one practitioner to pause, look again, and ensure that a neurodivergent person is not misunderstood but instead approached with greater understanding, then this book will have achieved what I hoped for.

The law in this book is accurate as of 1 December 2025.

*Natasha Khalique*
*December 2025*

# CONTENTS


| | | |
|---|---|---|
| Chapter One | Introduction | 1 |
| Chapter Two | My Journey and Perspective | 3 |
| Chapter Three | What Is Neurodivergence? | 11 |
| Chapter Four | Attention Deficit Hyperactivity Disorder (ADHD) | 21 |
| Chapter Five | Autism Spectrum Disorder/ Autism Spectrum Condition (ASD/ASC) | 45 |
| Chapter Six | Intersectionality and Neurodivergence | 57 |
| Chapter Seven | Legal Framework and Duties | 65 |
| Chapter Eight | Barriers to Participation | 75 |
| Chapter Nine | Representing a Neurodivergent Client | 81 |
| Chapter Ten | Neurodivergence in Public Law Proceedings | 100 |
| Chapter Eleven | Neurodivergence in Private Law Proceedings | 129 |

# CHAPTER ONE

# INTRODUCTION

Neurodiversity is a concept that is gaining greater recognition and discussion in today's society. The concept itself is not a new phenomenon. Human brains have always worked in diverse ways. However, the way in which we talk about it has dramatically changed in recent years. Terms such as "neurodiversity", "neurodivergence" and "neurodivergent" are far more prevalent in everyday conversation. It is important not to mistake an increase in prevalence of language for a deeper understanding. There is still a significant degree of misunderstanding and confusion about what neurodivergence is. Too often, it's dismissed as a passing trend, or minimised and misrepresented as a justification for poor behaviour. This lack of knowledge and understanding can have profound consequences, particularly when these misconceptions intersect with the family justice system.

The purpose of this book is to move beyond buzzwords, misconceptions and tick-box approaches. It seeks to explain what neurodivergence is, and just as importantly, what it is not. Designed both as an introduction and a practical reference, it encourages coordinated thinking about how neurodivergence should be recognised within the structures and practices of the family justice system. Bridging the gap between misunderstanding and reality is the essential first step towards creating a fairer, more informed and accessible process for everyone involved.

I write this not only as a family law barrister but also as someone who is neurodivergent. Living with both autism and attention deficit hyperactivity disorder (ADHD), I understand what it feels like to be misunderstood. I have experienced the diagnostic journey first-hand and have had to navigate systems that were not designed with the neurodivergent brain in mind. I also live the daily realities of being neurodivergent, including both its strengths and its challenges. My lived experience, combined with my professional work in the family courts, gives me a dual perspective and places me in a unique position. I can see the structural barriers that exist while also understanding, on a personal level, what it is like for neurodivergent individuals to navigate and overcome them. Drawing on this, I provide real-life examples and context to help interpret behaviours, presentations and patterns that are often misread without a neurodivergent lens.

This book is not designed to be a glossary of terms or a checklist of diagnostic criteria. Instead, it is intended to be a single place where practitioners can find legal frameworks, step-by-step guidance, practical tips and points to consider when challenges arise. By the end of this book, it is hoped that practitioners will feel more assured and confident in recognising when neurodivergence is a key issue, understanding how it might present and adapting the approach taken to better support neurodivergent individuals.

# CHAPTER TWO

# MY JOURNEY AND PERSPECTIVE

Why am I sharing my own journey? Neurodivergence does not discriminate. It can affect anyone, in any family, across every ethnicity and gender, and in ways both visible and invisible. Too often, when we read about neurodivergence in professional or academic contexts, the material feels detached. Traits are listed like symptoms to observe rather than experiences to live. But behind every label is a person whose story began long before any diagnosis was made. This is mine. I share it because lived experience is what brings understanding to life. Because a lack of awareness breeds assumptions, and assumptions can quietly shape the course of a person's life. By sharing my journey, I hope to bring that human element to light and to show how being neurodivergent has shaped me, how misunderstanding has impacted me, and how awareness can change everything.

I have often been told, "*You don't look autistic,*" or "*You don't seem like someone with ADHD.*" Neurodivergence doesn't have a look. In reality, I have both ADHD and autism. Comments like these reflect the risk of stereotypes and misconceptions about what neurodivergence should look like. The external may appear one way, but the internal experience can be entirely different. Looks can be deceiving. Neurodivergence is far more nuanced and multifaceted than meets the eye and taking it at face value risks individuals being left unseen, unsupported and misunderstood.

## Childhood

My earliest memories of feeling different go back to the age of five. I was academically bright and a high achiever, yet I constantly battled with anxiety. My Year 1 school report said, *"Natasha prefers the extracurricular activities."* I wasn't the obvious naughty or fidgety child. In fact, I was quite the opposite, the high performer, naturally academically bright, the school prefect and the Hermione Granger of my class. I could understand logic, patterns, and reasoning with ease, yet abstract comprehension wasn't so straightforward. I couldn't just "read between the lines." I remember doing the Key Stage 2 SATs and looking up around the room to see everyone writing away. I read words without retaining them and kept glancing back at the text thinking, "*This time it will go in*".

I developed unusual fascinations with things like cash tills, orthodontics, and braces. These interests had no obvious pattern, but I was fascinated by them. I wasn't interested in the Pokémon cards or collecting football stickers in the playground. I would rehearse conversations repeatedly, running through scenarios in my head because I was so worried about getting them wrong. Sensory sensitivities were also a distinct feature which shaped daily life. I struggled with certain foods and needed my food to be arranged in certain ways. I disliked uneven textures such as jellyfish or scars, which would send a physical shudder down my back and my nervous system into disarray. I felt overwhelmed by loud noises and crowded places.

One memory stands out vividly. I was five years old on sports day. My race partner and I had practised the novelty race over and over, and every time we won. On the actual day, we didn't. I was devastated. I cried so much that I missed the singles race because I couldn't just "bounce back". To everyone else it looked like I was a spoilt child or a sore loser who was used to being top in the class and couldn't cope with losing. But for me, it wasn't that. This was incomprehensible. We had practised, and the outcome had always been the same. I couldn't process how something so predictable could suddenly change. My world was black and white, and

I couldn't understand. That moment, though small to others, was my first real encounter with emotional dysregulation. My emotions were so intense that no amount of soothing or comforting from my parents or teachers could calm me down.

### Teenage years

As a teenager, the differences became more pronounced, and masking was at its peak. The emotional and physical effort required to hide my true self was exhausting, leaving me drained and often disconnected from who I really was. I continued to perform well academically, but planning revision schedules and sticking to routines was notoriously difficult. I procrastinated until the very last moment, then crammed everything in a single burst of energy, staying up all night. Reports described me as capable but inconsistent. Comments like *"Natasha has great ideas but does not put the work in"* missed the truth entirely. What looked like carelessness was executive dysfunction. I got an E in my GCSE English Literature mock but an A* in the final exam. Everyone was shocked, and I even got accused of cheating by my teacher. What people didn't realise was that I needed extra tuition weekly for a year with a tutor who understood my literal way of thinking and provided the support that I needed to overcome the barriers.

At fifteen, I tried to explain my struggles to a medical professional with the support of my parents. I drew a picture of my brain, shaded three-quarters of it, showed it to the doctor and said, "*The shaded part of my brain is struggling with concentration, and I can't focus*". I explained this wasn't always the case as when there was something I was really interested in; I could concentrate for hours. This was the first time I had found a way to articulate what was happening inside. Her response was, *"Perhaps higher education isn't for you"*. The shame and guilt that I felt sitting with my parents and hearing that comment was a new low. I felt sick and my limbs went numb from anxiety. I left the appointment with the doctor suggesting that I may be depressed and should consider trying an antidepressant.

I wanted to be a doctor at the time, had my GCSEs coming up and thought to myself, "*Where do I go from here?*". I remember sitting there, feeling unseen. I knew I had potential, but I couldn't translate it into consistent performance. No one could explain why. I internalised that sense of failure and carried it with me for years. I learned to mask, to keep up appearances, to appear fine even when I was unravelling inside. Inside, I felt a growing sense of isolation and frustration. It was akin to grieving my lost potential.

What followed was years of surviving and crashing in cycles. Periods of intense focus and achievement followed by burnout and withdrawal during exams. I pushed myself to meet expectations, desperate to prove that I was capable, but the cost was always high. I had three offers for medical school but missed my offer by two marks. I blamed myself. I simply wasn't good enough and maybe the medical professional was right, maybe higher education wasn't for me. The rejection sensitivity dysphoria that came from this was immense. I ended up doing Biology at University and then would apply for graduate medicine. That same cycle of last-minute cramming, all-nighters, and the immense mental, emotional and physical stress I put myself through continued. I would aim for perfectionism out of fear of failure but that in itself was unrealistic. I would have the best will in the world to start early, be more prepared and create revision plans next time but I came to accept that I worked better under pressure.

Sport became a huge outlet. It helped drown out the negative talk, both internal and external. I didn't feel the need to mask, could just be me and found a way to release my frustration. I played tennis competitively and ran marathons. I even signed up for a triathlon without having done any training and purchased a bike two days before the event. I completed it in 1 hour 15 minutes.

## Adulthood

Over the years, my understanding of myself has improved and I am more aware of what works and what doesn't work. However, I still encounter difficulties in my career and day-to-day life. I was sometimes described as difficult to manage and colleagues said I challenged authority, when in truth, I simply needed to understand before I could accept. My brain could not settle for half-answers. What others saw as argument and challenging authority, I saw as clarity-seeking so I could join the metaphorical dots up in my head, so I understood the bigger picture.

A senior, aware of my ADHD diagnosis, threatened to terminate my training citing that I had "*difficulties with communication and social skills*". It was even proposed that I have sessions with the senior to teach me these skills. Another said that I was using my neurodivergence as an excuse. When I explained that I prefer to drive rather than use public transport due to my sensory overwhelm, I was told that not everyone has a car and that I was to get on the train if I had to. I was labelled a "diva".

I was told I was too sensitive when comments disguised as banter left me upset and that I lacked social skills when I left events early rather than staying into the early hours. My social battery was depleted, and I needed to recharge. Preserving energy to attend court for the next day was survival, not rudeness. Even my hyperfocus was misunderstood. When I became absorbed in work, it was labelled as obsession or greed. When I made the decision to move back to Manchester from Liverpool, this was described as impulsive and that I was easily influenced by others. The reality was I had lived in Manchester before, and it was familiarity. It was my safe space where my nervous system was regulated, I was closer to my support network and it gave me the clear and very literal space between my work and home life.

There was a national shortage of ADHD medication and I had to ration what little medication I had left. This was an incredibly difficult period for many who have ADHD. It was in the news and media. People were taking time off work as sick leave as they were struggling. When I informed a senior of the situation her response was "*Oh, we all have bad days.*" Words like these cut deeper than they appear. They are dismissals of something unseen but profoundly real. What I thought was a positive by sharing my ADHD diagnosis, had completely backfired and compounded the feeling of impostor syndrome, not being good enough and the need to mask again. I was left in utter disbelief and shock that it was now being weaponised and used against me. At first, I was open about my ADHD diagnosis, but I decided not to disclose my autism diagnosis due to these encounters.

These experiences reveal a fundamental truth: when difference is met with judgment instead of curiosity, we lose the opportunity to learn from the very perspectives that drive progress. Labelling someone as "difficult," "too sensitive," or "a diva" silences the deeper truth of their experience and dismisses the adaptations that allow them to function in a world not built for their neurotype. What is often misread as defiance, sensitivity, or impulsivity is, in fact, a person navigating complexity with integrity, self-awareness, and resilience. The cost of misunderstanding is high, not only for the individual whose authenticity is punished, but for workplaces and communities that forfeit the richness of diverse minds. True inclusion demands that we stop labelling and start listening, that we move from tolerance to understanding, from judgment to empathy, and from stereotype to genuine human connection.

### Diagnosis and discovery

My ADHD diagnosis came during lockdown in 2020, when my younger sister lived with me for the first time. She saw how I could know exactly what I needed to do yet feel paralysed by the thought of starting. It wasn't laziness. It was executive dysfunction, being so overwhelmed that doing nothing felt safer than failing to do something and not knowing where to begin.

I resisted medication at first. I told myself I had survived thirty years without it, so why start now? But curiosity won, and I tried Concerta.

The side effects were intense, almost disorienting, as though I was watching myself from outside my body. Then I switched to Elvanse, and everything changed. It was as if a fog lifted. For the first time, I could sit and complete a task from start to finish. I remember sitting at the kitchen table and saying to my mum, *"I've actually finished my to-do list."* It was a simple sentence, but to me it felt like euphoric freedom. I cried. Was this what "normal" felt like?

My autism diagnosis followed during a medication review. As I described my difficulties in social settings, the doctor gently asked, *"Have you ever been assessed for autism?"* I hadn't. But within months, I was in the middle of an assessment and was diagnosed as being autistic.

**Reflection**

Neurodivergence matters because it challenges the narrow definition of "normal" that has long dictated who succeeds, who is understood, and who is left behind. It asks us to reimagine intelligence, communication, and success through a broader and more compassionate lens. Every neurodivergent mind holds a unique constellation of strengths such as creativity, depth, intuition, persistence, and insight, yet these are too often overshadowed by systems built for sameness. Understanding neurodivergence is not about pity or exception making; it is about equity, humanity, and progress. When society creates space for neurodivergent people to thrive everyone benefits, as workplaces become more innovative, relationships more authentic, and communities more inclusive. True inclusion begins when we stop asking neurodivergent people to shrink themselves to fit in and start expanding our understanding to fit them. Neurodivergence is not a flaw to be fixed; it is a form of brilliance that, when embraced, transforms the world around it.

# CHAPTER THREE

# WHAT IS NEURODIVERGENCE?

## Introduction

Neurodivergence is an umbrella term used to describe a range of neurodevelopmental conditions. In straightforward terms, it refers to the natural variations in the human brain that affect sociability, learning, attention, mood and other cognitive functions. Rather than framing these variations as deficits or disorders, the concept of neurodivergence recognises them as valuable forms of human diversity (Armstrong, 2017).

Individuals described as neurodivergent may include those with diagnoses such as autism spectrum disorder (ASD), attention deficit hyperactivity disorder (ADHD), dyslexia, dyspraxia, dyscalculia and Tourette syndrome. Importantly, neurodivergence is not a medical diagnosis but a perspective that reframes difference as diversity rather than deficit.

The concept of neurodivergence is based on the understanding that there is no single correct way for the human brain to function. Human minds vary in how they process information, regulate emotions and engage with the world. This stands in contrast with neurotypicality. Neurotypicality refers to individuals whose cognitive functioning aligns more closely with socially constructed norms.

In recent years, there has been a significant increase in public attention to neurodivergence, particularly autism and ADHD. Within the United Kingdom (UK), referrals for diagnostic assessments have risen sharply, waiting times have lengthened, and increasing numbers of adults are receiving diagnoses later in life (NHS England, 2025). This trend reflects not only a growing demand for clinical services but also a wider societal shift towards an improved understanding, acceptance and recognition of neurodivergent experiences. Most importantly, archaic myths and misconceptions are being challenged, and the outdated narrative is undergoing redefinition.

## Terminology

As discussions surrounding neurodivergence develop, so does the language used to describe it. Terms such as *neurodiversity*, *neurodivergence* and *neurotypical* are now more widely recognised, but they are often applied inconsistently or misunderstood. Within the legal context, unclear or inaccurate terminology can lead to confusion, miscommunication and flawed assumptions about an individual's needs and abilities. Clarity of language is essential for accurate understanding. The following key terms are defined below and are used throughout this book:

**Neurotypical**: An individual whose development and behaviour align with socially constructed norms.

**Neurodivergent**: An individual whose cognitive functioning diverges from these expectations.

**Neurodivergence**: An umbrella term covering Autism, ADHD, dyslexia, dyspraxia, dyscalculia, and Tourette syndrome.

**Neurodiversity**: The natural variation in cognitive functioning across humans (Armstrong, 2017).

## Neurodevelopmental conditions

### Autism Spectrum Disorder/ Autism Spectrum Condition (ASD/ASC)

ASD/ASC is characterised by differences in social communication, sensory processing, social interaction and the presence of repetitive and restrictive patterns of behaviour. Current estimates suggest that it affects approximately 1 in 100 people in the UK, which equates to approximately 1% of the UK population (National Autistic Society). However, it is suspected that the true prevalence is likely to be higher when undiagnosed individuals are taken into account. A more detailed exploration of ASD/ASC and its relevance within the family justice system is provided in Chapter 5.

### Attention Deficit Hyperactivity Disorder (ADHD)

ADHD is a neurodevelopmental condition characterised by inattention, impulsivity, and hyperactivity. Prevalence estimates have varied, with earlier figures suggesting that around 8% of the UK population may be affected (ADHD Aware, 2023). However, data published by NHS England in 2025 indicates that the true prevalence is closer to 5% in children and between 2–3% in adults (NHS England, 2025). ADHD is associated with difficulties in executive functioning such as planning, organisation and sustained focus. Strengths include creativity, adaptability, and problem-solving. A more detailed analysis of ADHD and its implications for participation within the family justice system is provided in Chapter 4.

### Dyslexia

Dyslexia is defined by the British Dyslexia Association as a "specific learning difficulty that primarily affects the skills involved in accurate and fluent word reading and spelling. Characteristic features are difficulties in phonological awareness, verbal memory and verbal processing speed" (BDA, 2023). Dyslexia is one of the most common neurodevelopmental conditions, affecting approximately 10% of the UK population, with around 4% experiencing more severe forms (British Dyslexia Association, 2024; Dyslexia UK, 2025). It is primarily characterised by persistent difficulties in reading, writing, and spelling.

### Dyspraxia (Developmental Coordination Disorder)

Dyspraxia, also referred to as Developmental Coordination Disorder (DCD), is a neurodevelopmental condition defined as a "significant impairment in the development of motor coordination, which interferes with academic achievement and activities of daily living" (American Psychiatric Association, 2013). It is estimated that it affects between 5–6% of school-aged children in the UK (Dyspraxia Foundation, 2023). Children and adults with dyspraxia may face challenges with handwriting, sports, and fine motor tasks, as well as broader challenges of organisation and time management (Hewitt, 2025).

### Dyscalculia

Dyscalculia affects a person's ability to understand and work with numerical information. It affects approximately 5–6% of the UK population (British Dyslexia Association, 2025; Dyslexia UK, 2025). It is characterised by difficulties in understanding numbers, performing arithmetic, and applying mathematical concepts to daily life tasks such as money management and timekeeping.

Although less widely recognised than dyslexia, dyscalculia can significantly impact education and employment outcomes. Research in educational neuroscience has highlighted how dyscalculia is associated with distinct patterns of neural processing differences rather than a lack of cognitive ability (Butterworth, Varma and Laurillard, 2011). Many individuals with dyscalculia excel in creative fields, verbal reasoning and spatial analysis.

## Tourette syndrome

Tourette syndrome is a neurological condition defined by the presence of both motor and vocal tics, typically with onset in childhood. Data from the NHS suggests that around 1% of school-aged children in the UK are affected (NHS, 2024). Symptom severity may fluctuate and often diminishes during adolescence, with approximately 80% of individuals experiencing improvement or remission by adulthood (Robertson, Eapen and Singer, 2009).

Tourette syndrome frequently coexists with other neurodevelopmental conditions such as ADHD and obsessive-compulsive disorder (OCD). Although such co-occurrence can present functional and social challenges, many individuals with Tourette syndrome also demonstrate notable strengths, including creativity, perseverance and cognitive flexibility.

## Deficit-based and strengths-based lenses

It is evident that there are a wide range of neurodevelopmental conditions. These may exist either in isolation or can co-occur within any individual. Each condition presents a distinct profile of cognitive functioning, often combining valuable strengths with areas of challenge. The interplay between multiple conditions can be complex and highly individual, influencing how a person experiences the world.

The conceptual lens through which neurodivergence is analysed and perceived is important. A deficit-based lens tends to highlight what a person can't do and emphasises areas of limitation. This often reinforces stereotypes, stigma and negative connotations. A strengths-based lens, in contrast, acknowledges challenges but also highlights abilities, adaptive skills and strategies and meaningful contributions. The same behaviour can appear very different depending on which perspective is applied.

This distinction between a deficit and strengths-based lens is especially important when looking at it in the context of the family court. Assessments of parenting capacity and decisions about a child's welfare may be shaped by how a parent's behaviour is interpreted. For example, challenges with executive functioning, sensory processing or social communication may be misread as disengagement, non-compliance or inadequate parenting, when in reality they may reflect neurodivergent differences that can be supported or reasonably accommodated.

The following table illustrates how certain behaviours, when viewed through a deficit-based lens, may be misinterpreted within family court proceedings, and how a strengths-based perspective can provide a more accurate and constructive understanding, particularly when assessing parenting capacity and participation.

| Example | Deficit-Based Lens | Strengths-Based or Balanced Lens |
| --- | --- | --- |
| ADHD – organisation | Parent is disorganised, misses appointments and cannot manage routines | Parent experiences difficulties with organisation but responds well to structured reminders and support systems |
| Autism – communication | Parent is socially awkward, unresponsive and struggles to communicate | Parent communicates differently, often preferring direct exchanges. With adjustments, they can provide reliable information |

| | | |
|---|---|---|
| ADHD – emotional regulation | Parent is volatile and unable to manage emotions appropriately | Parent experiences strong emotions but shows empathy and benefits from clear de-escalation strategies |
| Autism – parenting style | Parent is rigid, lacks warmth and struggles to adapt to children's needs | Parent provides predictability and structure, which benefits children. With support, they manage unexpected changes |
| Compliance with court orders | Parent fails to comply with directions due to irresponsibility | Parent finds paperwork and deadlines difficult but complies when tasks are broken down and support is provided |

Adopting a strengths-based or balanced perspective does not deny the existence of challenges, but it ensures that the full picture of an individual's abilities and potential is recognised. This shift in perspective is essential for fair and informed decision-making within the family justice system.

**References**

American Psychiatric Association (2013) *Diagnostic and statistical manual of mental disorders: DSM-5*. 5th edn. Washington, DC: American Psychiatric Publishing.

ADHD Aware (2023) *Neurodiversity and other conditions*. Available at: https://adhdaware.org.uk/what-is-adhd/neurodiversity-and-other-conditions/

British Dyslexia Association (2024) *Dyslexia prevalence*. Available at: https://www.bdadyslexia.org.uk/dyslexia

British Dyslexia Association (2023) *What is dyslexia?* Available at: https://www.bdadyslexia.org.uk/dyslexia/about-dyslexia/what-is-dyslexia

British Dyslexia Association (2025) *Dyscalculia prevalence*. Available at: https://www.bdadyslexia.org.uk/dyscalculia/how-can-i-identify-dyscalculia

Butterworth, B., Varma, S. and Laurillard, D. (2011) 'Dyscalculia: from brain to education', *Science*, 332(6033), pp. 1049–1053.

Dyslexia UK (2025) *How common are dyslexia and dyscalculia in the UK?* Available at: https://www.dyslexiauk.co.uk/how-common-are-dyslexia-and-dyscalculia-in-the-uk-updated-2024/

Dyspraxia Foundation (2023) *What is dyspraxia?* Available at: https://dyspraxiafoundation.org.uk/about-dyspraxia/

Hewitt, L. (2025) 'Developmental coordination disorder: A review and update', *Journal of Primary Care & Community Health*, 16, pp. 1–8.

Lingam, R., Hunt, L., Golding, J., Jongmans, M. and Emond, A. (2009) 'Prevalence of developmental coordination disorder using the DSM-IV at 7 years of age: a UK population-based study', *Pediatrics*, 123(4), pp. e693–e700.

Mentally Healthy Schools (2023) *Neurodiversity*. Available at: https://www.mentallyhealthyschools.org.uk/factors-that-impact-mental-health/vulnerable-children/neurodiversity/

National Autistic Society (n.d.) *What is autism? More than one in 100 people are autistic and there are at least 700,000 autistic adults and children in the UK.* Available at: https://www.autism.org.uk/advice-and-guidance/what-is-autism

NHS (2024) *Tourette's syndrome.* Available at: https://www.nhs.uk/conditions/tourettes-syndrome

NHS England (2025) *Report of the Independent ADHD Taskforce Part 1.* Available at: https://www.england.nhs.uk/long-read/report-of-the-independent-adhd-taskforce-part-1/

Robertson, M.M., Eapen, V. and Singer, H.S. (2009) 'The Tourette syndrome triad: Autism, ADHD and OCD', *International Review of Neurobiology*, 89, pp. 65–85.

Steenbergen, B., et al. (2024) 'Awareness about developmental coordination disorder', *Frontiers in Public Health*, 12, Article 1357921.

Taylor, J., Smith, A. and Brown, P. (2025) 'Toward a consensus on dyslexia: findings from a Delphi study', *Journal of Child Psychology and Psychiatry*, advance online publication.

University of Edinburgh (2023) *Neurodiversity Support.* Available at: https://equality-diversity.ed.ac.uk/disabled-staff-support/neurodiversity-support

Zwicker, J.G. (2012) 'Developmental coordination disorder: A review and update', *Developmental Medicine & Child Neurology*, 54(1), pp. 54–63.

# CHAPTER FOUR

# ATTENTION DEFICIT HYPERACTIVITY DISORDER (ADHD)

**What is ADHD?**

The National Institute for Health and Care Excellence (NICE) defines ADHD as *"a behavioural disorder with symptoms of hyperactivity, impulsivity, and inattention"* (NICE, 2019). ADHD is classified as a neurodevelopmental condition, meaning that differences in brain development during childhood influence physical, cognitive, emotional, and social functioning across life.

**ADHD prevalence and statistics in the UK**

It is estimated that around three million people in the UK are affected by ADHD, including approximately 623,000 children and 1.875 million adults (ADHD UK). NHS England estimates that around 2.5 million people may have ADHD, including undiagnosed cases, of which 741,000 are children and young people aged 5–24 years (NHS Digital, 2025).

Despite these high prevalence estimates, there is a marked disparity between the number of diagnosed cases and the number of undiagnosed individuals. Current NHS data shows that over 800,000 people have a formal ADHD diagnosis in England, equating to approximately 1 in 44 children and 1 in 125 adults recorded on GP systems (The Times, 2025). However, this figure is thought to represent only about one-third of the true ADHD population, with the remainder undiagnosed (Financial Times, 2025).

Prevalence varies by age group. ADHD affects an estimated 5% of children and 3–4% of adults in the UK (NHS England, 2025; The King's Fund, 2024). Diagnosis rates have risen significantly over the past two decades, particularly among boys aged 10–16 years. Prevalence in this age group increased from 1.4% in 2000 to 3.5% in 2018 (UCL, 2023).

The prevalence of ADHD has risen sharply in recent years. NHS England estimates that approximately 2,498,000 people in England are currently affected by ADHD, including those without a formal diagnosis, with 741,000 aged between 5 and 24 years (NHS Digital, 2025). Demand for assessments continues to escalate. As of June 2025, there were 491,470 open referrals for possible ADHD diagnosis in England, of which 337,095 (68.6%) were adults and 154,365 (31.4%) were children or young people (House of Commons Library, 2025). Among those awaiting assessment, 65.8% of adults and 62.2% of children had been on waiting lists for more than one year (House of Commons Library, 2025).

These extensive delays highlight the mounting pressure on diagnostic and treatment services, reflecting both greater public recognition of ADHD and systemic capacity challenges. The resulting backlog has significant social and psychological consequences, often exacerbating mental health difficulties, family stress, and educational and judicial inequalities (The Guardian, 2025b; Financial Times, 2025).

### Causes of ADHD

There is no single cause of ADHD. Research consistently demonstrates a strong genetic component, with heritability estimated at 74% (Faraone and Larsson, 2019). Environmental influences also contribute and include prenatal exposure to nicotine, alcohol or illicit substances, premature birth, low birth weight and early exposure to heavy metals (Banerjee, Middleton and Faraone, 2007). These factors interact with genetic predisposition rather than acting in isolation.

## What ADHD is not

It is important to dispel common myths and debunk widespread misconceptions about ADHD. ADHD is not caused by poor parenting, sugar, laziness, excessive screen time, or lack of discipline. It is simply not "naughty boy syndrome," nor is it a social trend or TikTok hype. Comments such as "we are all a bit ADHD" trivialise the real challenges that people with ADHD encounter. Within family law, such misconceptions risk parents being unfairly judged as irresponsible or neglectful and children being labelled as defiant rather than supported as neurodivergent (Young et al., 2020).

## Types of ADHD

NICE identifies three clinical presentations of ADHD (NICE, 2019):

**Inattentive presentation** involves persistent difficulties with focus, organisation, and memory. Children may lose belongings, forget instructions, or appear withdrawn. Adults may miss appointments, misplace items, and struggle with task initiation. Symptoms of inattentive ADHD are less outwardly disruptive. This can result in ADHD being overlooked or misattributed to daydreaming, lack of motivation, or anxiety. Such misattributions often contribute to delayed recognition and diagnosis (Young et al., 2020).

**Hyperactive–impulsive presentation** is more visible and is characterised by restlessness, fidgeting, excessive talking, interrupting and impulsive action. Children may fidget, climb inappropriately, interrupt, or act without considering danger. Adults may talk excessively, finish other people's sentences, and experience restlessness or racing thoughts. These behaviours are often misread as misbehaviour or rudeness rather than neurological differences (Cortese et al., 2018).

**Combined presentation** is the most common type of ADHD. It is characterised by symptoms of both inattention and hyperactivity–impulsivity.

### Presentation of ADHD traits: General, childhood, and adulthood

Although ADHD symptoms arise from the same underlying attentional and executive function differences, their outward presentation can vary by type and change over time. The tables below summarise general characteristics of ADHD and illustrate how these traits may appear in childhood compared to adulthood.

| Category | General Traits of ADHD |
|---|---|
| **Attention & Focus** | Short attention span for routine or unstimulating tasks<br>Difficulty sustaining focus; easily distracted by surroundings or thoughts<br>Failing to pay attention to detail (making 'careless mistakes')<br>Frequently losing track of what one is doing mid-task<br>Starting projects with enthusiasm but struggling to finish them<br>Periods of hyperfocus on areas of strong interest |
| **Organisation & Productivity** | Disorganisation with time, tasks, or belongings<br>Forgetfulness in daily life (appointments, items, deadlines)<br>Trouble following through on plans or multi-step instructions<br>Procrastination followed by intense last-minute effort<br>Difficulty prioritising tasks, everything feels urgent, or nothing does |

| | |
|---|---|
| **Executive Function & Memory** | Time blindness, poor sense of how long things take, losing track of time<br>Difficulty transitioning between tasks or stopping once engaged<br>Working memory challenges — forgetting steps, instructions, or intentions<br>Out of sight, out of mind tendencies (object permanence struggles) |
| **Hyperactivity** | Physical restlessness, fidgeting, or constant movement<br>Feeling 'driven by a motor,' difficulty relaxing or sitting still<br>Talking excessively or finding it hard to engage quietly<br>Mental hyperactivity, racing thoughts, difficulty switching off<br>Sleep difficulties (delayed sleep cycles, trouble winding down) |
| **Impulsivity & Behaviour** | Acting quickly without weighing consequences<br>Risk-taking behaviours (spending, driving, social risks)<br>Blurting things out, interrupting others<br>Impatience and difficulty waiting turns<br>Impulsive decision-making and inconsistent routines |
| **Emotional Regulation** | Emotional dysregulation, quick shifts in mood, frustration, or overwhelm<br>Rejection sensitivity (feeling criticism very deeply)<br>Low tolerance for boredom, delays, or setbacks<br>Shame, guilt, or perfectionism developed as coping responses<br>Low self-esteem from years of feeling 'different' or 'not enough' |

| | |
|---|---|
| **Sensory & Physical Regulation** | Heightened sensitivity to noise, light, textures, or temperature<br>Need for sensory stimulation (doodling, tapping, chewing, movement)<br>Difficulty maintaining regular energy levels (cycles of burnout and bursts of energy) |
| **Social & Interpersonal** | Talking a lot when excited, sometimes oversharing<br>Inconsistent communication (forgetting to reply, then sending long enthusiastic messages)<br>Struggles with authority, rigid systems, or unstructured environments<br>Masking or camouflaging difficulties to 'fit in' socially |

| Category | Common Traits of ADHD in Children |
|---|---|
| **Attention & Focus** | • Easily distracted by sights, sounds, or thoughts<br>• Makes careless mistakes in schoolwork<br>• Starts tasks but struggles to finish<br>• Short attention span for instructions or homework |
| **Organisation & Productivity** | • Frequently loses toys, books, or homework<br>• Forgets instructions<br>• Difficulty following multi-step directions |
| **Executive Function & Memory** | • Poor sense of time (5 minutes feels like 1 hour)<br>• Needs frequent reminders<br>• Forgets rules or steps in a task |

| | |
|---|---|
| **Hyperactivity** | • Fidgeting or squirming<br>• Runs/climbs in inappropriate places<br>• Talks excessively or interrupts play<br>• Struggles to sit still at meals or in class |
| **Impulsivity & Behaviour** | • Blurts out answers<br>• Interrupts conversations<br>• Difficulty waiting turns<br>• Acts without considering danger (e.g., running into the street) |
| **Emotional Regulation** | • Meltdowns, tantrums or outbursts<br>• Sensitive to criticism or being told off<br>• Difficulty calming down after being dysregulated |
| **Sensory & Physical Regulation** | • Sensitive to clothing textures, noise, or lights<br>• Chews on pencils/clothes<br>• Periods of high energy and activity followed by exhaustion |
| **Social & Interpersonal** | • Talks a lot when excited<br>• May dominate games or play<br>• Struggles with taking turns<br>• Can be perceived as bossy or "too much" by peers |

| Category | Common Traits of ADHD in Adults |
|---|---|
| Attention & Focus | • Struggles to concentrate in long meetings<br>• Zones out during conversations<br>• Starts projects but struggles to finish<br>• Makes small mistakes in reports/emails<br>• Hyperfocuses on one task and forgets others |
| Organisation & Productivity | • Desk, inbox, or calendar is cluttered<br>• Forgets appointments or double-books<br>• Leaves tasks until last minute<br>• Struggles to prioritise; jumps between tasks |
| Executive Function & Memory | • Poor time management; late to meetings<br>• Underestimates how long tasks take<br>• Forgets why they walked into a room<br>• Misses key project steps and deadlines<br>• Difficulty multitasking or procrastinating due to executive function freeze |
| Hyperactivity | • Fidgets with pen, taps feet, shifts in chair<br>• Talks quickly or dominates discussions<br>• Struggles in long training sessions<br>• Restless energy; paces or multitasks socially |
| Impulsivity & Behaviour | • Interrupts colleagues mid-sentence<br>• Blurts out ideas without thinking<br>• Impulsive spending (lunch, shopping)<br>• Makes quick decisions, later regrets them |

| | |
|---|---|
| **Emotional Regulation** | • Frustration when projects stall<br>• Sensitive to criticism or feedback<br>• Mood swings at work or socially<br>• Over-apologises or masks emotions |
| **Sensory & Physical Regulation** | • Overwhelmed by noise, lights, crowds<br>• Seeks stimulation (snacking, scrolling)<br>• Energy crashes after intense workdays<br>• Struggles with sleep routines |
| **Social & Interpersonal** | • Overshares in casual chats<br>• Inconsistent communication (ignores messages, then overcompensates)<br>• Struggles with rigid hierarchies<br>• Friendships intense but short-lived |

**ADHD in girls and women**

The stereotype of ADHD as "naughty boy syndrome" contributes to underdiagnosis of girls and women. Females are more likely to present with inattentive features such as shyness, daydreaming, perfectionism, people-pleasing, and anxiety, rather than overt hyperactivity (Young et al., 2020). This internalised presentation is less visible to teachers and professionals.

Girls frequently mask symptoms by overcompensating, which increases their risk of burnout, low self-esteem, and co-occurring anxiety or depression (Rucklidge, 2010). Research has shown that women with ADHD are more likely to be misdiagnosed with depression or anxiety and prescribed antidepressants. Whilst this may reduce secondary symptoms, it fails to address the core ADHD symptoms (The Lancet Psychiatry, 2024).

Hormones also play a role. Hormonal changes across the menstrual cycle, pregnancy, postpartum and menopause influence ADHD symptoms. A large study found that women with ADHD reported significantly higher rates of premenstrual dysphoric disorder (45% vs. 28% in the general population) and postpartum depression (58% vs. 19%) (de Jong et al., 2020). These hormonal influences should be considered in assessments and support planning, as they can exacerbate the challenges that ADHD can present.

Studies have also shown that women with ADHD are more likely to engage in risky sexual behaviours, experience unplanned pregnancies, and face higher risk of sexual victimisation (BMC Women's Health, 2024). These vulnerabilities must be understood in safeguarding and family law contexts.

## Functional traits of ADHD and their impact

### Organisation and procrastination

Organisation difficulties are a hallmark of ADHD. Adults may live in cluttered environments, forget deadlines, or double-book appointments. Parents may lose school forms, misplace uniforms, or forget appointments with professionals. Procrastination often results from task initiation difficulties. Individuals may delay starting a task until the pressure of a deadline forces action, creating cycles of last-minute panic (Sirois, Melia-Gordon and Pychyl, 2013). These behaviours can be misinterpreted as being irresponsible or not caring, when in fact they reflect executive function impairments (Barkley, Murphy and Fischer, 2006).

### Rejection Sensitivity Dysphoria (RSD)

Rejection sensitivity dysphoria (RSD) describes intense emotional responses to perceived criticism or rejection. Children may experience disproportionate distress when reprimanded by teachers. Adults may withdraw from relationships, processes or respond with anger when criticised. For parents, feedback from social workers may trigger visible upset, which risks being misinterpreted as instability, hostility or even being aggressive (Dodson, 2019).

### Jobs and employment

Employment outcomes for people with ADHD are consistently poorer when compared to neurotypicals. Adults with ADHD are twice as likely to be unemployed, and when employed, earn approximately 17% less than their peers (de Graaf et al., 2008). Frequent job changes, disciplinary dismissals, and underemployment are common (Barkley et al., 2006). This instability contributes to financial insecurity.

### Sleep

Sleep disturbance is common, with delayed sleep onset, irregular patterns, and unrefreshing sleep (Bijlenga et al., 2019). Poor sleep worsens inattention, impulsivity, and mood regulation. For children, lack of sleep can lead to school and behavioural difficulties. For adults, it reduces resilience and parenting capacity. Sleep difficulties should therefore be considered in welfare assessments.

### Substance misuse and coping strategies

ADHD is strongly associated with substance misuse, with up to 25% of adults with ADHD reporting problems with drugs or alcohol (Kessler et al., 2006). Many describe using substances as a form of self-medication to manage attention or emotional distress. Other maladaptive coping strategies include compulsive spending, overeating, or excessive gaming. In family law, substance misuse is often scrutinised; understanding its link with ADHD is essential to avoid pathologising without addressing the underlying reasons.

## Relationships

Children with ADHD are more likely to experience peer rejection and loneliness (Hoza, 2007). Adults often face volatile romantic relationships characterised by impulsive decision-making, inconsistent communication, or conflict (Canela et al., 2017). In family disputes, such relationship histories may be unfairly used to question parental stability unless contextualised as part of the parents' ADHD profile.

## Mental health and ADHD

### Social anxiety and anxiety disorders

Children with ADHD are more likely to develop social anxiety due to peer rejection and criticism. Adults often internalise these experiences, leading to avoidance of social situations (Sciberras et al., 2014). Anxiety disorders co-occur in up to 50% of individuals with ADHD (Katzman et al., 2017). In family proceedings, this may appear as hesitancy, withdrawal during meetings or disengagement from proceedings.

### Depression

Depression affects 30–40% of individuals with ADHD (Meinzer et al., 2013). The repeated experience of failure and rejection contributes to low mood and hopelessness. Women are particularly at risk due to underdiagnosis and misdiagnosis (Young et al., 2020).

### Self-harm and suicide

Adolescents with ADHD are significantly more likely to engage in self-harm, with estimates as high as 20% (Hinshaw et al., 2012). Suicide risk is also elevated, with ADHD more than doubling the risk of attempts (James, Lai and Dahl, 2020). In family law, disclosure of self-harm or suicidality must be treated with sensitivity and contextualised within ADHD.

## Resilience

Despite these risks, resilience is possible. Positive family support, effective interventions, and recognition of strengths improve long-term outcomes (Miranda et al., 2015). In family law, highlighting resilience ensures that children and parents are not defined solely by vulnerabilities.

## Treatment and support

### Therapeutic interventions

NICE (2019) recommends psychoeducation for individuals with ADHD and their families. Cognitive behavioural therapy adapted for ADHD helps with procrastination, negative thinking, and emotional regulation (Knouse and Safren, 2010). ADHD coaching provides practical strategies for time management and organisation.

Parent training programmes improve routines and reduce stress (Daley et al., 2014). Occupational therapy can address sensory issues in children. School-based support, such as individual education plans, is essential to prevent exclusion.

### Medication

In the UK, stimulant medication constitutes the first line of pharmacological treatment for ADHD. Methylphenidate (commercially available as Ritalin, Concerta XL and Medikinet) is the most commonly prescribed agent, with lisdexamfetamine (Elvanse) and dexamfetamine (Dexedrine) also utilised. Non-stimulant alternatives include atomoxetine (Strattera) and guanfacine (Intuniv) (Bolea Alamañac et al.,

2014). These medications can enhance attention, reduce impulsivity and stabilise behavioural regulation, although they do not constitute a curative intervention. Decisions regarding the initiation of medication are individual and should be informed by clinical assessment and patient preference.

Within the context of family law, access to appropriate treatment is highly relevant when evaluating parental capacity and engagement with proceedings. Parents with untreated ADHD may present as inconsistent, disorganised or emotionally dysregulated, whereas those receiving effective treatment and supportive interventions such as ADHD-specific coaching may function well. It is important that the court does not equate untreated difficulties with parental incapacity but instead considers systemic barriers to timely assessment, diagnosis and access to treatment when interpreting presentation and participation.

## Adverse Childhood Experiences and ADHD

Children with ADHD are at increased risk of experiencing Adverse Childhood Experiences (ACEs). This can include abuse, neglect, parental conflict and household instability. These early adversities can exacerbate ADHD symptoms, particularly impulsivity and emotional dysregulation (Brown et al., 2017). A US study found that children with four or more ACEs were more than three times as likely to be diagnosed with ADHD (Bitsko et al., 2018).

Practitioners must be aware of the bidirectional relationship: ADHD may shape a child's coping responses to trauma, while traumatic experiences can amplify ADHD-related difficulties and obscure accurate diagnosis. It is crucial to distinguish the impact of trauma from that of underlying neurodevelopmental conditions. Trauma related hypervigilance, impulsivity and attentional difficulties may be misconstrued as solely behavioural in nature, while the impulsivity and emotional dysregulation characteristic of ADHD may heighten a child's vulnerability to maltreatment and family breakdown.

Accurate differentiation between the effects of trauma and the manifestations of ADHD is critical when assessing risk, parenting capacity and the best interests of the child. Misattributing neurodevelopmental symptoms to defiance or poor parenting can lead to unjust conclusions regarding parental adequacy. Overlooking trauma may result in an incomplete formulation of the child's needs. Recognition of the bidirectional relationship between ACEs and ADHD supports more informed decision-making, enabling tailored care plans, appropriate therapeutic interventions and proportionate expectations of a child's behavioural capacity. Such analysis helps to safeguard against both under-protection and over-intervention, ensuring that orders and care arrangements are responsive to the child's neurodevelopmental profile and trauma history.

## The economic and social cost of untreated ADHD

Untreated ADHD costs the UK an estimated £20 billion per year, including healthcare, education, lost productivity, and criminal justice involvement (Le et al., 2014). Children with ADHD are disproportionately excluded from school. In 2018, pupils with special educational needs accounted for 43% of exclusions but only 15% of the population (DfE, 2019). Adults with untreated ADHD face higher unemployment and reduced earnings (de Graaf et al., 2008). This means that families affected by ADHD may face systemic disadvantages in education, employment, and finances.

## ADHD and family law

Misunderstanding ADHD in family proceedings risks unjust outcomes. Parenting assessments may conflate disorganisation with neglect, emotional dysregulation with volatility, or late attendance with disinterest. Children with ADHD may be labelled as defiant or unmanageable rather than supported.

Courts must also consider the impact of ADHD on access to justice. Parents with ADHD may struggle with lengthy documents, complex orders, or rigid deadlines. Without reasonable adjustments, they are at risk of procedural unfairness.

## ADHD, Parenting After Separation, and Contact

Post-separation parenting requires organisation and reliability. For parents with ADHD, difficulties with time blindness and memory can make contact handovers challenging. Research shows that inconsistent routines increase distress for children with ADHD (Harvey et al., 2011). Missed contact may be unfairly read as lack of interest when it reflects executive dysfunction.

Practical supports such as shared digital calendars, reminders, and neutral handover points can enable parents to maintain consistent contact. Courts should recognise that with support, parents with ADHD can sustain positive and reliable relationships.

## Parenting strengths associated with ADHD

Parents with ADHD often bring enthusiasm, playfulness, and creativity into their family life (Mahdi et al., 2017). Many describe being deeply empathetic towards their children, particularly if the child is also neurodivergent. Qualitative research shows that children value their parents' spontaneity and imaginative play (Shanahan et al., 2011).

Highlighting these strengths ensures a balanced assessment of parenting capacity. ADHD does not equate to incapacity; rather, with recognition and support, parents with ADHD can provide safe and nurturing environments.

## Practical checklist for practitioners

Practitioners can use the following tick-box list to guide their work with clients who have ADHD:

- ☐ Have I considered whether ADHD may be present in the child or parent?
- ☐ Am I distinguishing between ADHD traits and assumptions of irresponsibility or neglect?
- ☐ Have I adapted communication by giving clear, concise instructions in both written and verbal form?
- ☐ Have I considered reasonable adjustments, such as reminders or extended deadlines, to enable fair participation in proceedings?
- ☐ Am I interpreting emotional dysregulation within the context of ADHD rather than as hostility or aggression?
- ☐ Have I considered the high rates of co-occurring conditions such as anxiety, depression, and substance misuse?
- ☐ Am I aware of the specific challenges for women with ADHD, including hormonal influences and masking?
- ☐ Have I recognised and documented the strengths of parents with ADHD, such as creativity and empathy, alongside challenges?
- ☐ Have I taken into account how adverse childhood experiences may interact with ADHD in children and parents?

☐ Do I have sufficient training on ADHD, and if not, have I sought guidance or referred to specialists?

## References

All Party Parliamentary Group on ADHD (2021) *The Forgotten Crisis: ADHD Waiting Times in the UK.* London: APPG on ADHD.

Armstrong, T. (2010) *Neurodiversity: Discovering the Extraordinary Gifts of Autism, ADHD, Dyslexia, and Other Brain Differences.* Cambridge, MA: Da Capo Press.

Banerjee, T. D., Middleton, F. and Faraone, S. V. (2007) Environmental risk factors for attention deficit hyperactivity disorder. *Acta Paediatrica,* 96(9), pp.1269–1274.

Barkley, R. A., Murphy, K. R. and Fischer, M. (2006) *ADHD in Adults: What the Science Says.* New York: Guilford Press.

Biederman, J., Faraone, S. V., Spencer, T. et al. (1995) Patterns of psychiatric comorbidity, cognition, and psychosocial functioning in adults with attention deficit hyperactivity disorder. *American Journal of Psychiatry,* 152(11), pp.1792–1798.

Bijlenga, D., Vollebregt, M. A., Kooij, J. J. S. and Arns, M. (2019) The role of the circadian system in the etiology and pathophysiology of ADHD: Time to redefine ADHD? *Attention Deficit and Hyperactivity Disorders,* 11(1), pp.5–19.

Bitsko, R. H., Holbrook, J. R., Ghandour, R. M. et al. (2018) Epidemiology and impact of health care provider diagnosed ADHD and comorbidities among US children, 2016. *Journal of Developmental and Behavioral Pediatrics,* 39(9), pp.735–746.

Bolea-Alamañac, B., Nutt, D. J., Adamou, M. et al. (2014) Evidence-based guidelines for the pharmacological management of attention deficit hyperactivity disorder: Update on recommendations from the British Association for Psychopharmacology. *Journal of Psychopharmacology*, 28(3), pp.179–203.

Brown, N. M., Brown, S. N., Briggs, R. D. et al. (2017) Associations between adverse childhood experiences and ADHD diagnosis and severity. *Academic Pediatrics*, 17(4), pp.349–355.

Canela, C., Buadze, A., Dube, A. et al. (2017) Experiences of partners of adults with ADHD: A qualitative study. *International Journal of Environmental Research and Public Health*, 14(5), p.450.

Chronis-Tuscano, A., Clarke, T. L., O'Brien, K. A. et al. (2011) Parent ADHD and evidence-based treatment for their children: Review and directions for future research. *Journal of Child Psychology and Psychiatry*, 52(3), pp.220–231.

Cortese, S., Kelly, C., Chabernaud, C. et al. (2018) Toward systems neuroscience of ADHD: A meta-analysis of 55 fMRI studies. *American Journal of Psychiatry*, 169(10), pp.1038–1055.

Daley, D., van der Oord, S., Ferrin, M. et al. (2014) Behavioral interventions in attention deficit hyperactivity disorder: A meta-analysis of randomized controlled trials across multiple outcome domains. *Journal of the American Academy of Child and Adolescent Psychiatry*, 53(8), pp.835–847.

de Graaf, R., Kessler, R. C., Fayyad, J. et al. (2008) The prevalence and effects of adult attention deficit hyperactivity disorder (ADHD) on the performance of workers: Results from the WHO World Mental Health Survey Initiative. *Occupational and Environmental Medicine*, 65(12), pp.835–842.

de Jong, L., Hartman, C. A., Kuiper, D. et al. (2020) Hormonal influences on ADHD symptoms in women: A clinical perspective. *Journal of Psychiatric Research*, 123, pp.56–63.

Department for Education (2019) *Permanent and Fixed Period Exclusions in England 2017 to 2018*. London: DfE.

Dodson, W. (2019) Rejection sensitivity in adults with ADHD. *ADHD Report*, 27(1), pp.1–8.

Faraone, S. V. and Larsson, H. (2019) Genetics of attention deficit hyperactivity disorder. *Molecular Psychiatry*, 24(4), pp.562–575.

Harvey, E. A., Danforth, J. S., McKee, T. E. et al. (2011) Parenting of children with ADHD: Differential parenting and family relationships. *Journal of Abnormal Child Psychology*, 29(5), pp.373–383.

Hinshaw, S. P., Owens, E. B., Zalecki, C. et al. (2012) Prospective follow up of girls with attention deficit hyperactivity disorder into early adulthood: Continuing impairment includes elevated risk for suicide attempts and self-injury. *Journal of Consulting and Clinical Psychology*, 80(6), pp.1041–1051.

Hoza, B. (2007) Peer functioning in children with ADHD. *Journal of Pediatric Psychology*, 32(6), pp.655–663.

James, A., Lai, F. H. and Dahl, C. (2020) Attention deficit hyperactivity disorder and suicide: A systematic review. *European Child and Adolescent Psychiatry*, 29(11), pp.1501–1516.

Katzman, M. A., Bilkey, T. S., Chokka, P. et al. (2017) Adult ADHD and comorbid disorders: Clinical implications of a dimensional approach. *BMC Psychiatry*, 17, p.302.

Kessler, R. C., Adler, L., Barkley, R. et al. (2006) The prevalence and correlates of adult ADHD in the United States: Results from the

National Comorbidity Survey Replication. *American Journal of Psychiatry*, 163(4), pp.716–723.

Knouse, L. E. and Safren, S. A. (2010) Current status of cognitive behavioral therapy for adult attention deficit hyperactivity disorder. *Psychiatric Clinics of North America*, 33(3), pp.497–509.

Le, H. H., Hodgkins, P., Postma, M. J. et al. (2014) Economic impact of childhood/adolescent ADHD in a European setting: The Netherlands as a reference case. *European Child and Adolescent Psychiatry*, 23(7), pp.587–598.

Mahdi, S., Viljoen, M., Massuti, R. et al. (2017) An international qualitative study of ability and disability in ADHD using the WHO-ICF framework. *European Child and Adolescent Psychiatry*, 26(10), pp.1219–1231.

Meinzer, M. C., Pettit, J. W., Waxmonsky, J. G. et al. (2013) ADHD and long-term risk for depression: Longitudinal associations with parental monitoring and peer victimisation. *Journal of Abnormal Child Psychology*, 41(7), pp.1249–1259.

Miranda, A., Colomer, C., Fernández, M. I. et al. (2015) Predictors of resilience in children with ADHD. *Journal of Attention Disorders*, 19(7), pp.607–617.

NHS Digital (2022) *Mental Health of Children and Young People in England 2022*. London: NHS Digital.

NICE (2019) *Attention deficit hyperactivity disorder: diagnosis and management (NICE Guideline NG87)*. London: National Institute for Health and Care Excellence.

Quinn, P. O. and Madhoo, M. (2014) A review of attention deficit hyperactivity disorder in women and girls: Uncovering this hidden diagnosis. *The Primary Care Companion for CNS Disorders*, 16(3).

Rucklidge, J. J. (2010) Gender differences in attention deficit hyperactivity disorder. *Psychiatric Clinics of North America*, 33(2), pp.357–373.

Sayal, K., Prasad, V., Daley, D. et al. (2018) ADHD in children and young people: Prevalence, care pathways, and service provision. *The Lancet Psychiatry*, 5(2), pp.175–186.

Sciberras, E., Lycett, K., Efron, D. et al. (2014) Anxiety in children with ADHD: Relationships with family and peer functioning. *European Child and Adolescent Psychiatry*, 23(6), pp.555–564.

Shanahan, M. A., Pennington, B. F., Yerys, B. E. et al. (2011) Emotion regulation in children with ADHD. *Journal of Abnormal Child Psychology*, 39(7), pp.891–901.

Sirois, F. M., Melia-Gordon, M. L. and Pychyl, T. A. (2013) "I'll look after my health, later": An investigation of procrastination and health. *Personality and Individual Differences*, 55(6), pp.699–703.

The Lancet Psychiatry (2024) Gender disparities in diagnosis and treatment of ADHD. *The Lancet Psychiatry*, 11(2), pp.95–97.

White, H. A. and Shah, P. (2006) Uninhibited imaginations: Creativity in adults with ADHD. *Personality and Individual Differences*, 40(6), pp.1121–1131.

Young, S., Adamo, N., Ásgeirsdóttir, B. B. et al. (2020) Females with ADHD: An expert consensus statement taking a lifespan approach. *BMC Psychiatry*, 20, 404.

Young, S., Gudjonsson, G., Chitsabesan, P. et al. (2015) A meta-analysis of the prevalence of attention deficit hyperactivity disorder in incarcerated populations. *Psychological Medicine*, 45(2), pp.247–258.

ADHD UK (n.d.) *ADHD incidence.* Available at: https://adhduk.co.uk/adhd-incidence/

Financial Times (2025) *Almost 2.5mn people in England estimated to have ADHD.* 29 May. Available at: https://www.ft.com/content/a620597a-d36f-4fd2-9941-41784f807eb4

NHS Digital (2025) *MI ADHD: May 2025.* Available at: https://digital.nhs.uk/data-and-information/publications/statistical/mi-adhd/may-2025

NHS England (2025) *ADHD programme update.* Available at: https://www.england.nhs.uk/long-read/attention-deficit-hyperactivity-disorder-adhd-programme-update/

The Guardian (2025a) *ADHD prescriptions in England have risen by 18% each year since pandemic.* 11 March. Available at: https://www.theguardian.com/society/2025/mar/11/adhd-prescriptions-in-england-have-risen-by-18-each-year-since-pandemic

The Guardian (2025b) *NHS accused of "abject failure" on ADHD as 550,000 await assessment in England.* 29 May. Available at: https://www.theguardian.com/society/2025/may/29/up-to-25-million-people-in-england-could-have-adhd-says-nhs

The King's Fund (2024) *Adult ADHD: assessment, diagnosis, data and service provision.* Available at: https://www.kingsfund.org.uk/insight-and-analysis/reports/adult-adhd-assessments-diagnosis-data-service-provision

The Times (2025) *Formal diagnoses of ADHD in England reach 800,000.* Available at: https://www.thetimes.co.uk/article/formal-diagnoses-of-adhd-in-britain-hit-80000-n0ql8gjr3

UCL (2023) *Significant rise in ADHD diagnoses in the UK.* 11 July. Available at: https://www.ucl.ac.uk/news/2023/jul/significant-rise-adhd-diagnoses-uk

# CHAPTER FIVE

# AUTISM SPECTRUM DISORDER/AUTISM SPECTRUM CONDITION (ASD/ASC)

## What is ASD/ASC?

The National Institute for Health and Care Excellence (NICE) defines autism as a lifelong condition that affects how people communicate and interact, and how they perceive the world (NICE, 2021). Autism is classified as a neurodevelopmental condition, arising from differences in brain development that influence cognition, emotion, and behaviour across the lifespan.

The Diagnostic and Statistical Manual of Mental Disorders (DSM-5) consolidated several previously distinct diagnostic categories, including Asperger's syndrome, autistic disorder and pervasive developmental disorder not otherwise specified, into a single classification of ASD (American Psychiatric Association, 2013). The *International* Classification of Diseases (ICD-11) similarly conceptualises autism as a spectrum that encompasses a wide range of presentations and support needs (World Health Organization, 2019).

## ASD/ASC prevalence and statistics in the UK

Prevalence studies estimate that approximately 1–2% of the UK population are autistic (Brugha et al., 2016). NHS Digital (2022) reports that in England, approximately 120,000 children aged 5–19 have a current autism diagnosis. This equates to 1.8% of the age group. Among adults, research from UCL suggests that more than 1.2 million people in England may be autistic, nearly double previous figures, with as many as three-quarters remaining undiagnosed (UCL, 2023). Diagnosis rates remain higher in males, but growing evidence shows significant under-recognition in females.

## Causes of ASD/ASC

There is no single cause of autism. Twin studies show a heritability estimate of 50–90%, indicating a strong genetic influence (Tick et al., 2016). Specific genetic variations, including copy number variations and de novo mutations, have been identified (Sandin et al., 2017).

Environmental factors also play a contributory role when interacting with genetic predisposition. Examples of environmental factors include advanced parental age, very preterm birth, low birthweight, and prenatal exposure to valproate or maternal infections (Gardener, Spiegelman and Buka, 2011). These act in interplay with genetic susceptibility.

Importantly, large-scale studies have found no link between vaccines and autism, debunking a long-standing myth (Taylor, Swerdfeger and Eslick, 2014).

## What ASD/ASC is not

Autism is not a disease, mental illness, or the result of poor parenting. Discredited theories such as the "refrigerator mother hypothesis" have been thoroughly rejected. Autism is not the same as learning disability, although the two can co-occur. It is also inaccurate to equate autism with "being shy", "socially awkward" or "quirky". Such misconceptions carry real risks and can have significant consequences in legal contexts. For example, a child who has meltdowns due to sensory overload may be misinterpreted as defiant or being "behaviourally difficult". A parent who avoids eye contact may be viewed as deceptive, evasive and manipulative. Such misinterpretations can lead to unfair judgments if professionals lack the contextual understanding.

## The ASD/ASC spectrum: Communication and support needs

As the name suggests, autism is highly diverse in both presentation and support requirements. One of the clearest indicators of spectrum variability is language and communication ability. Approximately 25–35% of autistic children are minimally verbal or non-speaking by school age (Rose et al., 2016). These children may rely on alternative or augmentative communication systems, such as Picture Exchange Communication System (PECS), sign language, or electronic speech-generating devices. Being non-verbal does not equate to being non-communicating. Autistic individuals often express themselves through non-verbal means.

At the other end of the spectrum are verbally fluent autistic individuals who may have average or above-average intelligence. These individuals may mask or camouflage social difficulties by imitating neurotypical behaviours. While they may appear outwardly independent, many experience hidden distress, social exhaustion, and mental health difficulties as a result of masking (Hull et al., 2017).

Support needs also vary widely. Some autistic individuals require lifelong 24-hour care, while others live independently with minimal adjustments. For legal and safeguarding professionals in family law, this underscores the importance of individualised assessment rather than reliance on outdated and stigmatising labels such as "high functioning" or "low functioning". If an individual is "high functioning", this means that they have learned to mask to appear "normal" to the outside world. However, such individuals are at prime risk of their support needs being missed due to coping and/or masking strategies they have developed.

## Autism in boys

Autism has historically been associated with boys, partly because the earliest clinical research was based almost exclusively on male patients. Studies suggest that autism is diagnosed three to four times more often in boys than in girls (Loomes, Hull and Mandy, 2017). Boys are more likely to display overt behaviours such as aggression or highly visible repetitive movements, which tend to draw early attention from teachers and clinicians (Rutter, 2005).

As a result, boys are typically identified and diagnosed at a younger age than girls. One UK study found that the average age of diagnosis was 7 years for boys compared with 10 years for girls (Russell et al., 2015). Early recognition and diagnosis can facilitate access to educational support, but it also increases the risk of stigmatisation. Boys are more likely to be labelled as "problematic" and face exclusion. Department for Education data shows that autistic boys are overrepresented in exclusion statistics. Autistic pupils, the majority of whom are male, accounted for 29% of permanent exclusions of pupils with special educational needs in 2018 (DfE, 2019).

In family proceedings, this matters because a boy's disruptive behaviour may be interpreted as a result of poor parenting or neglect, when in fact it reflects unmet support needs.

## Autism in girls and women

Autism in females has historically been underdiagnosed. Girls are more likely to present with internalised features, such as perfectionism, social anxiety, or intense interests that align with socially acceptable topics (Lai and Szatmari, 2020). Many engage in masking or camouflaging, consciously imitating neurotypical behaviours to fit in socially. Masking can reduce outward visibility, but it contributes to exhaustion, anxiety, and depression (Hull et al., 2017).

Research suggests that for every three males diagnosed, at least one female remains undiagnosed (Loomes, Hull and Mandy, 2017). Late or missed diagnosis is associated with poorer mental health, reduced self-esteem, and increased risk of victimisation and vulnerability. Autistic women are also disproportionately at risk of sexual abuse, with one study finding that

78% had experienced sexual victimisation compared to 47% of non-autistic peers (Brown-Lavoie, Viecili and Weiss, 2014).

Failure to recognise the nuanced presentations of autism in females may lead to mothers being unfairly judged and autistic girls being overlooked during safeguarding or welfare assessments.

## Co-occurring conditions

Autism rarely occurs in isolation. Research indicates that 70–80% of autistic people have at least one additional co-occurring neurodevelopmental or mental health condition (Lai et al., 2019). Common co-occurrences include:

- **ADHD**: Present in up to 40% of autistic children (Antshel and Russo, 2019).
- **Epilepsy**: Occurs in 20–30% of autistic individuals, especially those with intellectual disability (Spence and Schneider, 2009).
- **Anxiety and depression**: Affect up to 50–70% of autistic adults (Hollocks et al., 2019).
- **Gastrointestinal issues**: Reported in up to 70% of children with autism (McElhanon et al., 2014).

For family law practitioners, recognising these co-occurring conditions is critical. A child with autism and ADHD may appear highly impulsive, while a parent with autism and depression may seem withdrawn. Without awareness, behaviours linked to co-occurring conditions may be wrongly attributed to neglect, non-engagement or incapacity.

## Bullying and victimisation

Autistic children are at significantly increased risk of bullying compared to their neurotypical peers. A US study found that 63% of autistic children had reported being bullied, compared to 30% of neurotypical peers (Zablotsky et al., 2014). In the UK, the National Autistic Society (2016) found that nearly 50% of autistic pupils had been bullied at school, contributing to higher exclusion rates.

Bullying increases risks of anxiety, depression, and school refusal. Within family law proceedings, reports of behavioural challenges must therefore be contextualised: disruptive behaviour may reflect peer victimisation rather than poor parenting.

## Transitions from childhood to adulthood

The transition from children's to adult services is widely recognised as a point of crisis. Many families report losing support once a child turns 18 years old. The National Autistic Society (2018) found that only 21% of autistic young people felt they had received adequate transition support. Poorly managed transitions are associated with unemployment, social isolation, and mental health difficulties.

For family courts, this is highly relevant in cases involving young autistic individuals leaving care and undergoing the transition between service providers. Breakdowns during transition often result from a lack of appropriate services and can present in fluctuations in presentation. The court and practitioners must be aware of this, particularly if this is a period during which assessments are taking place.

## Treatment and support

Autism is not a condition to be cured. It is a lifelong neurodevelopmental condition. Evidence-based interventions have been identified to enhance quality of life. NICE (2021) recommends the following as examples:

- Psychoeducation for families
- Speech and language therapy for communication
- Occupational therapy for sensory and motor challenges
- Cognitive Behavioural Therapy adapted for autism for anxiety and depression
- Parent training programmes, which improve family resilience

Autism is not treated with medication. However, pharmacological interventions may be appropriate for co-occurring conditions, including ADHD, anxiety, or epilepsy. Current best practice prioritises neurodiversity-affirming approaches that recognise strengths and address identified needs.

## Parenting strengths

Autistic parents bring unique strengths to family life. Research shows they often provide structure, predictability, and honesty, which can be protective factors (Crane et al., 2019). These qualities can be protective, especially when children are also neurodivergent (Crane et al., 2019). In the context of family proceedings, recognising such strengths is essential to avoid a one-sided assessment that focuses exclusively on perceived deficits.

## Practical checklist for practitioners

- ☐ Have I considered whether autism may be present in the child or parent, and sought specialist assessment if appropriate?
- ☐ Am I distinguishing between autistic traits and misinterpretations of evasiveness, defiance, or neglect?
- ☐ Have I considered co-occurring conditions that may influence behaviour?
- ☐ Am I mindful of the heightened risks of bullying, victimisation, and trauma in autistic children?
- ☐ Have I recognised health inequalities and the potential for unaddressed medical needs?
- ☐ Have I considered the additional vulnerabilities of autistic women and girls, including masking and risk of abuse?
- ☐ Have I factored in transition points, such as leaving school or care, which may trigger crises?
- ☐ Have I documented the strengths of autistic parents alongside challenges?
- ☐ Do I have sufficient training, or should I seek guidance from autism specialists?

## References

American Psychiatric Association (2013) *Diagnostic and Statistical Manual of Mental Disorders* (5th ed.). Washington, DC: APA.

Antshel, K. M. and Russo, N. (2019) Autism spectrum disorders and ADHD: Overlapping phenomenology, diagnostic issues, and treatment considerations. *Current Psychiatry Reports*, 21(5), p.34.

Brugha, T. S., Spiers, N., Bankart, J. et al. (2016) Epidemiology of autism in adults across age groups and ability levels. *British Journal of Psychiatry*, 209(6), pp.498–503.

Brown-Lavoie, S. M., Viecili, M. A. and Weiss, J. A. (2014) Sexual knowledge and victimisation in adults with autism spectrum disorders. *Journal of Autism and Developmental Disorders*, 44(9), pp.2185–2196.

Crane, L., Adams, F., Harper, G. et al. (2019) 'Something needs to change': Mental health experiences of young autistic adults in England. *Autism*, 23(2), pp.477–493.

Department for Education (2019) *Permanent and Fixed Period Exclusions in England 2017 to 2018*. London: DfE.

Gardener, H., Spiegelman, D. and Buka, S. L. (2011) Perinatal and neonatal risk factors for autism: A comprehensive meta-analysis. *Pediatrics*, 128(2), pp.344–355.

Hirvikoski, T., Mittendorfer-Rutz, E., Boman, M. et al. (2016) Premature mortality in autism spectrum disorder. *British Journal of Psychiatry*, 208(3), pp.232–238.

Hollocks, M. J., Lerh, J. W., Magiati, I. et al. (2019) Anxiety and depression in adults with autism spectrum disorder: A systematic review and meta-analysis. *Psychological Medicine*, 49(4), pp.559–572.

Hull, L., Mandy, W. and Petrides, K. V. (2017) Behavioural and cognitive sex/gender differences in autism spectrum condition and typically developing males and females. *Autism*, 21(6), pp.706–717.

Knapp, M., Romeo, R. and Beecham, J. (2009) Economic cost of autism in the UK. *Autism*, 13(3), pp.317–336.

Lai, M. C., Kassee, C., Besney, R. et al. (2019) Prevalence of co-occurring mental health diagnoses in the autism population: A systematic review and meta-analysis. *Lancet Psychiatry*, 6(10), pp.819–829.

Lai, M. C. and Szatmari, P. (2020) Sex and gender impacts on the behavioural presentation and recognition of autism. *Current Opinion in Psychiatry*, 33(2), pp.117–123.

LeDeR (2021) *The Learning Disabilities Mortality Review Annual Report 2021*. Bristol: University of Bristol.

Loomes, R., Hull, L. and Mandy, W. P. L. (2017) What is the male-to-female ratio in autism spectrum disorder? A systematic review and meta-analysis. *Journal of the American Academy of Child and Adolescent Psychiatry*, 56(6), pp.466–474.

Matson, J. L. and Kozlowski, A. M. (2011) The increasing prevalence of autism spectrum disorders. *Research in Autism Spectrum Disorders*, 5(1), pp.418–425.

McElhanon, B. O., McCracken, C., Karpen, S. and Sharp, W. G. (2014) Gastrointestinal symptoms in autism spectrum disorder: A meta-analysis. *Pediatrics*, 133(5), pp.872–883.

National Autistic Society (2016) *The Autism Employment Gap*. London: NAS.

National Autistic Society (2018) *Too Much Information: Transition to Adulthood*. London: NAS.

NHS Digital (2022) *Mental Health of Children and Young People in England 2022.* London: NHS Digital.

NICE (2021) *Autism spectrum disorder in under 19s: Support and management (NICE Guideline CG170).* London: National Institute for Health and Care Excellence.

Rose, V., Trembath, D., Keen, D. and Paynter, J. (2016) The proportion of minimally verbal children with autism spectrum disorder in a community-based sample. *Journal of Autism and Developmental Disorders*, 46(2), pp.697–706.

Russell, G., Ford, T., Steer, C. and Golding, J. (2015) Identification of children with autism spectrum disorder in a population sample. *Autism Research*, 8(3), pp.297–303.

Rutter, M. (2005) Autism research: Lessons from the past and prospects for the future. *Journal of Autism and Developmental Disorders*, 35(2), pp.241–257.

Sandin, S., Lichtenstein, P., Kuja-Halkola, R. et al. (2017) The heritability of autism spectrum disorder. *JAMA*, 318(12), pp.1182–1184.

Spence, S. J. and Schneider, M. T. (2009) The role of epilepsy and epileptiform EEGs in autism spectrum disorders. *Pediatric Research*, 65(6), pp.599–606.

# CHAPTER SIX

# INTERSECTIONALITY AND NEURODIVERGENCE

Intersectionality refers to the way that multiple and overlapping identities such as race, gender, class, sexuality, culture and disability interact to produce distinct experiences of privilege and discrimination. Within the context of neurodivergence, intersectionality is not merely theoretical but a lived reality that determines who is recognised, who is supported and, unfortunately, who is marginalised. Neurodivergent individuals face systemic barriers across education, healthcare and the justice system. These barriers intensify when neurodivergence coexists with other marginalised identities, particularly for women, racially minoritised groups and families in poverty. The consequences reverberate from childhood through adulthood and into the family justice system, where misunderstanding and misrecognition often lead to life-altering injustice.

## Mental health and neurodivergence

Mental health outcomes for autistic individuals and individuals with ADHD demonstrate a severe public health crisis. Studies show that between 11% and 66% of autistic adults experience suicidal thoughts and up to 35% have planned or attempted suicide (Bradley et al., 2021; Cassidy et al., 2014; Autistica, 2025). A meta-analysis by Moseley et al. (2023) reported that 34.2% of autistic adults without a co-occurring learning disability had experienced suicidal thoughts, and 24.3% had made attempts, highlighting the urgent need for supportive, accessible, and affirming mental health care for autistic people. Autistic children are 28 times more likely to consider or attempt suicide than their non-autistic peers (Royal College of Psychiatrists, 2021). Globally, there were approximately 13,400 excess suicide deaths among autistic individuals in

2021, accounting for 1.8% of all suicides (Cassidy et al., 2024). Coroner studies show that around 10% of those who died by suicide displayed elevated autistic traits, approximately 11 times the prevalence found in the general population (Cassidy et al., 2014).

Masking, a behaviour where neurodivergent individuals conceal traits to conform to social expectations, has been identified as a major contributor to psychological distress, depression and suicidal ideation (Bradley et al., 2021; National Autistic Society, 2024). Women and racially minoritised individuals are particularly prone to masking due to cultural and gendered expectations, leaving them invisible in diagnostic frameworks yet at heightened mental health risk.

### Educational disadvantage and the EHCP crisis

Educational inequality for neurodivergent children is now systemic. In January 2025, over 1.7 million pupils in England were identified as having special educational needs (SEN), representing 19.6% of the total school population (House of Commons Library, 2025). Among these, approximately 500,000 pupils (5.3%) had an Education, Health and Care Plan (EHCP), while 1.3 million (14.2%) received SEN support without a formal plan (UK Government, 2025). The number of pupils with an EHCP has more than doubled since 2016, reaching 638,700 active plans in 2025, a 10.8% increase from 2024 (UK Government, 2025). However, only 46.4% of new EHCPs were issued within the statutory 20-week timeframe (UK Government, 2025).

Autism remains the most common primary need among children with EHCPs, accounting for 33.6% of all plans. Other key categories include speech, language and communication needs (20.7%) and social, emotional and mental health difficulties (23.6%) (UK Government, 2024).

The socioeconomic divide remains stark. 43.8% of children with an EHCP and 39.3% of those receiving SEN support are eligible for free school meals, compared with only 22.2% of children without identified needs (UK Government, 2024). At ages sixteen to nineteen, pupils with EHCPs were on average 7.1 grades behind their peers, while those receiving SEN support were 3.7 grades behind (Parliamentary Office of Science and Technology, 2023).

The financial burden of these failings is immense. Between 2014 and 2023, the SEND funding deficit reached £3.3 billion, with forecasts projecting it will rise to £5 billion by 2026 (The Guardian, 2024). The National Audit Office (2024) reported that even though funding rose by 58% in real terms between 2014–15 and 2024–25 to £10.7 billion, the system remains financially unsustainable and fails to deliver improved outcomes. Local authorities are increasingly reliant on private specialist placements that cost an average of £62,000 per pupil per year, compared with £24,000 in state schools (Financial Times, 2025).

### Exclusion and the pathway to criminalisation

Children with SEN are disproportionately excluded from school. During the 2023–24 academic year, there were 10,900 permanent exclusions and 955,000 suspensions, representing increases of 16% and 21% respectively (Department for Education, 2024). Pupils with SEN were significantly overrepresented. Children eligible for free school meals were suspended at four times the rate of their peers and permanently excluded at five times the rate (Department for Education, 2024). For pupils with ADHD, the picture is even more concerning: 39% have experienced fixed-term exclusions and 11% have been permanently excluded. Within the prison population, 49% of men and 33% of women reported having been excluded from school (The SEN Expert, 2024).

## Ethnic and gender disparities in diagnosis

### Ethnic inequity

Diagnosis rates for autism and ADHD vary widely by ethnicity. A national study of seven million schoolchildren found autism prevalence to be highest among Black pupils (2.1%), compared with lower rates among White pupils and substantially lower rates among Roma and Irish Traveller pupils (0.85%) (Roman-Urrestarazu et al., 2021). Socioeconomic deprivation explained approximately 12% of the elevated diagnosis rates among Black and mixed ethnicity children. However, cultural and institutional biases often lead to late or missed diagnoses, with teachers and healthcare providers misattributing neurodivergent behaviours to discipline problems rather than neurological differences (The Guardian, 2024; The Voice, 2023).

### Gender inequity

Gender disparity remains pronounced. Autism has traditionally been diagnosed four to five times more often in boys than in girls (Brugha et al., 2011). Recent meta-analysis suggests the true ratio may be closer to 3:1 (Loomes et al., 2017). Rutherford et al. (2022) estimated that up to 80% of autistic females remain undiagnosed by the age of 18. Girls are typically diagnosed 1.8 years later than boys, often only during adolescence, as they are more likely to mask their challenges to conform socially (Harrop et al., 2024). Diagnostic criteria remain biased towards male behavioural patterns, contributing to chronic under-recognition.

## References

Autism Education Trust (2011) *Autism: A guide for criminal justice professionals – Part 1: Learning materials.* Department for Education.

Bradley, L., Shaw, R., Baron-Cohen, S. and Cassidy, S. (2021) 'Autistic adults' experiences of camouflaging and its perceived impact on mental health', *Autism in Adulthood*, 3(4), pp. 320–329. doi:10.1089/aut.2020.0079.

Brugha, T., Cooper, S.A., McManus, S. and Purdon, S. (2011) *Autism spectrum disorders in adults living in households throughout England: Report from the Adult Psychiatric Morbidity Survey 2007.* Leeds: The NHS Information Centre.

Cassidy, S. et al. (2014) 'Suicidal ideation and suicide plans or attempts in adults with Asperger's syndrome attending a specialist diagnostic clinic: a clinical cohort study', *The Lancet Psychiatry*, 1(2), pp. 142–147. doi:10.1016/S2215-0366(14)70248-2.

Cassidy, S. et al. (2024) 'Autism and suicide: global estimates of premature mortality', *Psychiatry Research*, 329, 115431. doi:10.1016/j.psychres.2024.115431.

Clarke, L., McKay, E. and Brown, C. (2025) 'Intersectionality and disability: A scoping review', *Social Sciences*, 14(9), 176. doi:10.3390/socsci14090176.

Daley, D. and Birchwood, J. (2010) 'ADHD and academic performance', *Child: Care, Health and Development*, 36(4), pp. 455–464. doi:10.1111/j.1365-2214.2009.01046.x.

Department for Education (2024) *Permanent and fixed-period exclusions in England: 2023/24.* London: DfE.

Ethnicity Facts and Figures (2021) *UK population by ethnicity – national and regional populations.* London: Cabinet Office.

Family Justice Council (2025) *Guidance on neurodiversity in the Family Justice System for practitioners* London: FJC.

Harrop, C., Jones, R. and Simonoff, E. (2024) 'Are diagnostic rates of autistic females increasing?', *Journal of Child Psychology and Psychiatry*, 65(5), pp. 566–579. doi:10.1111/jcpp.13505.

House of Commons Library (2025) *FAQ: ADHD statistics (England).* London: House of Commons Library.

Loomes, R., Hull, L. and Mandy, W. (2017) 'What is the male-to-female ratio in autism spectrum disorder? A systematic review and meta-analysis', *Journal of Child Psychology and Psychiatry*, 58(9), pp. 1087–1095. doi:10.1111/jcpp.12689.

Moseley, R. L., Gregory, J. D., Smith, P. and Baron-Cohen, S. (2023) 'Suicidality in autistic people: meta-analyses', *Molecular Autism*, 14(1), 11. doi:10.1186/s13229-023-00544-7.

NAO (2024) *Support for children and young people with special educational needs.* London: National Audit Office.

National Autistic Society (2024) *Masking: understanding autistic experiences.* Available at: https://www.autism.org.uk/advice-and-guidance/topics/behaviour/masking

National Institute for Health and Care Excellence (2019) *Attention deficit hyperactivity disorder: diagnosis and management (NG87).* London: NICE.

NHS England Digital (2025) *ADHD Management Information – May 2025.* London: NHS England.

Parliamentary Office of Science and Technology (2023) *Special educational needs and disabilities.* London: POST.

Roman-Urrestarazu, A. et al. (2021) 'Autism prevalence and risk by ethnic group in England', *JAMA Pediatrics*, 175(9), pp. 928–936. doi:10.1001/jamapediatrics.2021.1145.

Royal College of Psychiatrists (2017) *Blame it on the brain? Exploring ADHD as a criminogenic factor.* London: RCPsych.

Royal College of Psychiatrists (2021) *Suicide and autism.* London: RCPsych.

Rutherford, M. et al. (2022) 'Gender disparities in autism diagnosis', *Frontiers in Psychology*, 13, 887003. doi:10.3389/fpsyg.2022.887003.

The Guardian (2024) 'UK Black children face cultural barriers to accessing help with autism and ADHD', *The Guardian*, 31 March.

The Guardian (2024) 'Spiralling demand and shrinking budgets: why England's SEND system is buckling', *The Guardian*, 22 December.

The Times (2024) 'SEND and autism costs surge to £12 billion', *The Times*, 14 July.

The Voice (2023) 'Black special needs kids failed by schools', *The Voice Online*, 3 March.

UK Government (2024) *Special educational needs and disability analysis and summary of data sources – August 2024.* London: Department for Education.

UK Government (2025) *Education, health and care plans, England: 2025.* London: Department for Education.

The SEN Expert (2024) *ADHD and exclusions.* Available at: https://www.thesenexpert.co.uk/blog/adhd-and-exclusions

# CHAPTER SEVEN

# LEGAL FRAMEWORK

The legal framework governing the participation of neurodivergent individuals in family proceedings is principally shaped by three sources: the Equality Act 2010, the Family Procedure Rules 2010 (FPR), and Practice Direction 3AA (PD3AA). It is important to be familiar with these and to have them at your fingertips.

## The Equality Act 2010 and the Duty of Reasonable Adjustments

The Equality Act 2010 provides the primary legislative protection for individuals against discrimination, harassment and victimisation because of protected characteristics, including disability.

Section 6 defines disability as *'a physical or mental impairment, and the impairment has a substantial and long-term adverse effect on an individual's ability to carry out normal day-to-day activities'* (Equality Act 2010, s.6). This definition encompasses a wide range of neurodevelopmental conditions including ASD/ASC, ADHD, dyslexia and dyspraxia.

Section 20 imposes a proactive duty on public bodies, including the Family Court, to make reasonable adjustments for an individual who has a disability. The duty extends to:

- Adjusting provisions, criteria or practices that place the person at a disadvantage (s.20(3)),
- Making alterations to physical features that create barriers (s.20(4))
- Providing auxiliary aids or services where necessary (s.20(5))

Failure to make reasonable adjustments amounts to unlawful discrimination under s.21 (Equality Act 2010). In the family justice context, these adjustments may take the form of participation directions such as ground rules hearings, adapted questioning, intermediaries, breaks, or giving evidence remotely. These measures are intended to ensure understanding, reduce disadvantage, and support more meaningful engagement. Ultimately, this ensures fairness and compliance with Article 6 of the European Convention on Human Rights (ECHR) (Barnes, 2020; George, 2021).

## The Family Procedure Rules 2010 and access to justice

Part 3A of the Family Procedure Rules (FPR), together with Practice Direction 3AA (PD3AA), establishes a clear framework for ensuring that vulnerable individuals can participate effectively in proceedings and provide their best evidence.

The rules and practice direction impose a duty on the court to identify vulnerability, consider its impact, and make appropriate participation directions. For neurodivergent parents and children, these safeguards are critical in protecting rights under Article 6 ECHR (fair trial) and Article 8 ECHR (right to family life).

## Overriding objective and case management duties

The Family Procedure Rules 2010 (FPR) provide the procedural framework for family cases. Rule 1.1 sets out the overriding objective of dealing with cases justly, including ensuring parties are on an equal footing and can participate fully. Rule 1.4 imposes a duty on the court to actively manage cases, which includes identifying vulnerability at the earliest stage. Part 3A of the FPR and Practice Direction 3AA provide detailed guidance on vulnerability and participation directions.

### Court's mandatory duty to consider vulnerability

Rule 3A.9 requires the court to consider the issue of vulnerability from the inception until the conclusion of proceedings. Under r.3A.4 and r.3A.5, the court must consider whether a party's participation or the quality of their evidence is likely to be diminished by vulnerability, and if so, must consider whether participation directions are necessary.

### Purpose and approach in PD3AA

PD3AA, para 1.2, states: '*The objective of this Practice Direction is to ensure a fair hearing by providing for appropriate measures to be put in place to assist vulnerable parties and witnesses to participate in proceedings and to give evidence.*' It emphasises early identification of vulnerability, the potential need for expert or cognitive assessments, and the use of the Advocate's Gateway toolkits. PD3AA, paragraph 5.2 further states: '*The court should consider all possible measures, including intermediaries, special questioning techniques, breaks, and adaptations to language, in order to secure effective participation.*'

### Mandatory checklist of vulnerability factors (Rule 3A.7)

Rule 3A.7 sets out a mandatory checklist of factors when the court is considering participation directions. These include:

- Intimidation or controlling behaviour
- Mental disorder or impairment of intelligence/social functioning
- Physical disability or medical treatment
- Age, maturity, and understanding

- Social, cultural, and religious background
- Domestic circumstances
- Nature of the issues, including abuse
- Availability and cost of measures

**Possible measures the court can order (Rule 3A.8)**

The court may order measures contained within r.3A.8, which can be summarised as:

- Preventing a witness from seeing another party
- Use of live link (video evidence)
- Communication devices
- Appointment of an intermediary
- Other adaptations in PD3AA.

**Recording of participation directions**

Where the court has made, varied or revoked participation directions in respect of a vulnerable party, this must be recorded on the face of the order in accordance with r.3A.9.

## Applying Part 3A in practice

The following flowchart illustrates the practical steps to be applied by Part 3A and PD3AA. This process can assist practitioners in ensuring compliance and safeguarding procedural fairness.

## Flowchart: Applying Part 3A FPR in Family Proceedings

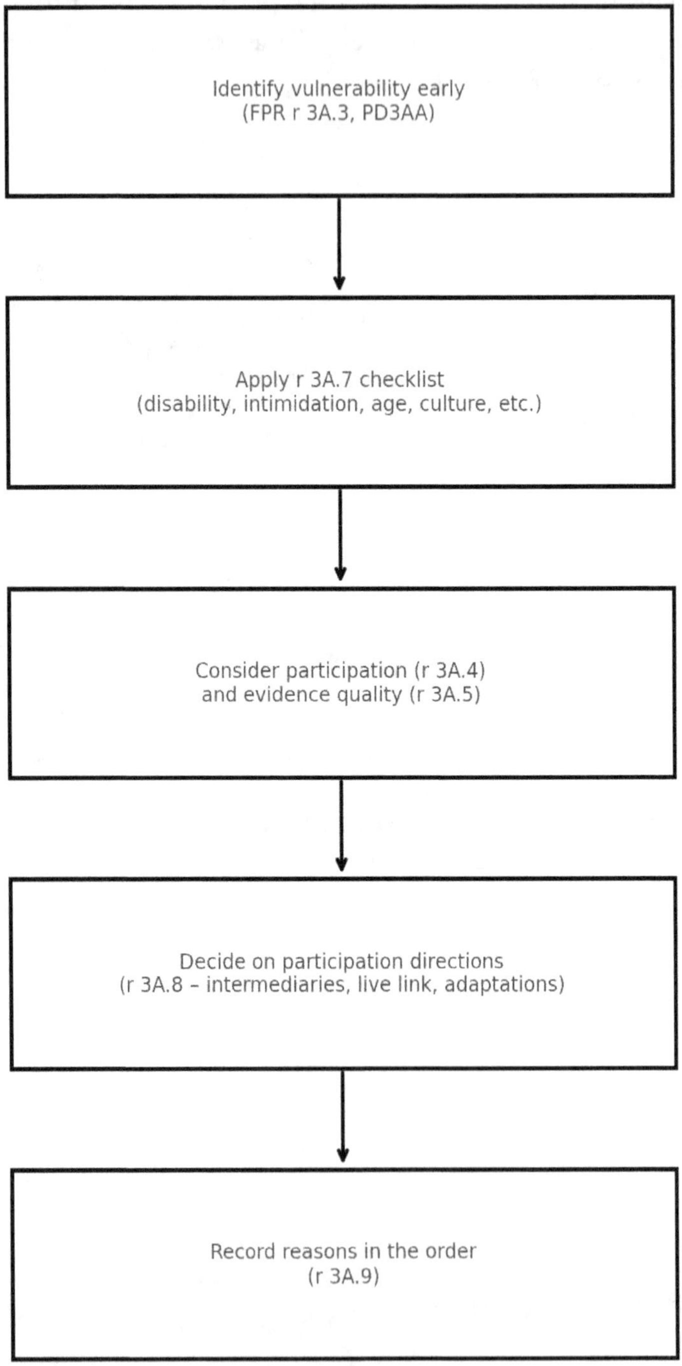

## Consequences of failing to apply Part 3A and PD3AA

A failure to apply Part 3A and PD3AA, through not recognising vulnerability and implementing appropriate measures, can have profound consequences for neurodivergent parties and witnesses. This inadvertently creates barriers to accessing justice. Failing to recognise and account for neurodivergence triggers a domino effect of disadvantage and harm.

The first and most fundamental barrier arises at the level of participation itself. Parents, children and witnesses are unable to participate meaningfully in proceedings if their communication, sensory, cognitive or emotional needs are not recognised and supported. Impaired participation then cascades into a wider denial of justice, where the voices, experiences and needs of neurodivergent individuals are either misunderstood, misinterpreted, minimised or overlooked altogether.

Such misunderstandings often result in unmet needs, overwhelm, a feeling of being misunderstood by the system, misplaced blame and emotional distress. This may be perceived by the court and professionals as disengagement or aggressive outbursts. This, in turn, causes deep and lasting trauma for neurodivergent individuals as they navigate a legal system that is intended to protect but instead inadvertently and unintentionally compounds their difficulties.

Ultimately, the failure to provide appropriate and reasonable adjustments leads to assessments and decisions being made on incomplete, inaccurate, or misinformed evidence. Each stage reinforces the next, creating a chain reaction of disadvantage. This may result in serious breaches of fundamental rights, including Article 6 and Article 8 of the ECHR. Article 6 provides an absolute right to a fair trial for all parties. Importantly, this right is not confined to the courtroom itself but extends across the entire litigation process. As Munby J (as he then was) stated in *Re L (Care: Assessment: Fair Trial)* [2002] 2 FLR 730 at [113]:

> *"The fair trial guaranteed by Article 6 is not confined to the purely judicial part of the proceedings. Unfairness at any stage of the litigation process may amount to a breach of Article 8 and Article 6. Article 6 rights are absolute: they cannot be watered down or qualified."*

Similarly, Article 8 ECHR protects the right to respect for family life, which the Family Court may only interfere with where it is both necessary and proportionate. When procedural barriers prevent neurodivergent parties or children from fully engaging with proceedings, any resulting orders may fail this test of proportionality and necessity.

Case law also makes clear that the adaptation of process is a judicial obligation rather than an optional courtesy. As Lady Justice Hallett stated in *R v Lubemba; R v JP* [2014] EWCA Crim 2064 at [45]:

> *"Advocates must adapt to the witness, not the other way round."*

This principle underscores the requirement for the family justice system to adapt to the needs of vulnerable participants, rather than expecting those participants to conform to processes that may inherently disadvantage them. The court's obligation to ensure a fair and accessible hearing therefore extends beyond the courtroom itself to include every stage of case management, assessment and evidence gathering.

Failure to comply with these duties risks procedural unfairness, the erosion of trust in the legal process, and potentially unlawful interference with family life. For practitioners and judges alike, recognising and applying the safeguards provided by Part 3A and PD3AA is essential to uphold both domestic legal obligations and international human rights standards.

## Practical checklist for practitioners

- ☐ Has vulnerability been flagged and identified at the earliest stage of proceedings (FPR r.3A.3)?
- ☐ Has the court applied the r.3A.7 checklist?
- ☐ Have you framed applications around the factors contained in r.3A.7 checklist. For example, highlight ADHD-related processing difficulties or autistic spectrum needs for structure and predictability?
- ☐ Has the court considered whether participation or the quality of evidence is likely to be diminished (r.3A.4–3A.5)?
- ☐ Has expert or cognitive assessment been directed where appropriate (PD3AA, para 3.6)?
- ☐ Have appropriate participation directions been made (r.3A.8), such as intermediaries, live link, or adapted questioning?
- ☐ Are decisions on vulnerability and participation directions clearly recorded in the order (r.3A.9)?
- ☐ If an intermediary is unavailable, propose alternative measures such as shorter sessions, visual aids, or adapted questioning. Record why the intermediary was necessary (r 3A.9(5)).
- ☐ Has the advocate used the Advocate's Gateway Toolkits and adapted communication accordingly (PD3AA, para 5.7)?

- ☐ Have all reasonable adjustments under the Equality Act 2010, s.20 been considered and implemented where necessary?

- ☐ Always invite the court to record explicitly whether r 3A.4 and r 3A.5 have been considered. Failure to do so risks an appeal on Article 6 grounds.

**References**

Barnes, C. (2020) Disability, Discrimination and the Law. London: Routledge.

Equality Act 2010. (2010) UK Public General Acts, c.15. Available at: https://www.legislation.gov.uk/ukpga/2010/15/part/2

Family Procedure Rules 2010, SI 2010/2955.

George, R. (2021) Vulnerability and Participation in Family Justice.

Family Law Journal, 51(2), pp.145–162.

Re M (A Child: Intermediaries) [2025] EWCA Civ 440.

Articles 6 and 8 of the European Convention on Human Rights.

# CHAPTER EIGHT

# BARRIERS TO PARTICIPATION

## An analogy of participation

Before turning to the practical challenges that neurodivergent individuals encounter, it may help to picture what participation actually feels like for many neurodivergent individuals. Imagine being handed a pair of 3D glasses at the cinema for a film designed to be seen in 3D. Without them, you can still watch, but the images are blurred, distorted, and incomplete. For many neurodivergent people, engaging with the family justice system without appropriate adjustments is much the same. They may be physically present and may try to participate, but they are denied the clarity and depth of understanding that justice requires. This is not simply a matter of comfort; it is about fairness, equality, and the protection of rights.

## Systemic barriers to fair participation: Key challenges faced by neurodivergent individuals

Just as watching a 3D film without glasses distorts the experience, gaps in the family justice system distort how neurodivergent individuals are perceived and treated. These barriers are not abstract. They have direct consequences for credibility assessments, parenting evaluations and, ultimately, decisions about their family life.

## Limited professional understanding

Professionals across the family justice system, whether social workers, solicitors or barristers, often have little grounding in neurodivergence. This is not a criticism, but reflects the fact that neurodivergence has only recently begun to receive wider societal recognition. Behaviours linked to autism, ADHD, dyslexia, or other conditions are therefore routinely misinterpreted. An autistic parent who avoids eye contact may be judged as evasive, while a parent with ADHD who struggles to meet paperwork deadlines may be perceived as careless or neglectful. These misinterpretations are far from neutral. They influence assessments of credibility, parenting capacity, and ultimately, decisions that determine whether children remain with their families. 61% of autistic adults reported that professionals did not communicate with them in ways they could understand (National Autistic Society, 2020).

## Lack of training and guidance

Despite the fact that between 15–20% of the UK population is neurodivergent (ONS, 2021; National Autistic Society, 2020), there is no compulsory training for judges, lawyers, or social workers. Where training does exist, it is voluntary and inconsistent, meaning outcomes can depend on the knowledge of the professional involved. The House of Commons Education Committee (2019) has highlighted how this lack of training perpetuates disadvantage.

## Court processes and unmet needs

Processes within the courts also fail to account for neurodivergence. Forms, directions, and frameworks rarely prompt professionals to consider whether a parent or child might be neurodivergent. When neurodivergence is not recognised or is overlooked, essential needs remain unmet. Assessments may be delayed or undertaken without bespoke reasonable adjustments. This leaves parents and children without the support they require. Research has shown that 74% of autistic children in care were placed with foster carers who had not received autism specific training (APPGA, 2017). In education, more than half of autistic children have been excluded at least once (Ambitious about Autism, 2018). These failures ripple into the justice system, where unmet needs are reframed as parental shortcomings.

## Communication barriers

Family courts rely heavily on written and spoken communication, yet very little is adapted for those who process information differently. Although tools such as "All About Me" profiles and Education, Health and Care Plans (EHCPs) exist, they are not consistently utilised. Research has found that only 12% of parents felt EHCP processes were clear and easy to understand (DfE, 2017). The lack of joined-up communication between professionals means that new teams often start from scratch, forcing parents to retell their story. This can be an exhausting, retraumatising and frustrating process. It also increases the risk that professionals rely on inconsistent or incomplete information.

## Courtroom engagement

Within the courtroom, participation can still present difficulties. While the law makes provision for vulnerable individuals to receive adjustments, in practice these are not necessarily applied consistently. As a result, neurodivergent individuals may at times depend on the awareness and discretion of the judge or advocate, rather than on clear and reliable safeguards. Alongside this, behaviours such as avoiding eye contact, needing additional time to process questions, using a fidget toy or presenting questions in a manner that differs from expected courtroom norms may be misinterpreted as evasive or uncooperative. These misunderstandings can have a direct impact on credibility and reliability.

## The impact of stigma

Stigma compounds these barriers. Neurodivergent people are too often labelled as “awkward”, “odd”, or “difficult”, terms which shape how they are perceived and treated. Such stigma directly undermines credibility and affects parenting assessments.

## Parental blame

The culture of parental blame reinforces these injustices. A child’s school refusal, which may stem from anxiety, can be reframed as parental neglect. Parents with disabilities, including neurodivergence, are more than twice as likely to have their children removed (Gordon et al., 2017). Once labelled as problematic, parents may avoid seeking help for fear of further scrutiny, perpetuating a cycle of non-support, escalation, and renewed involvement with child protection services. In November 2024, the Autism and Parental Blame Project identified that parents of autistic children are at higher risk of parental blame, child protection proceedings and are three times more likely to be accused of fabricated or induced illness compared to parents of neurotypical children.

## Consequences of failing to recognise neurodivergence

The consequences of failing to recognise neurodivergence can be far-reaching. Families may disengage not because they lack commitment or concern, but because they feel misunderstood, unsupported and unsafe within the process. When needs are overlooked, behaviours may be misinterpreted, and difficulties reframed as parental shortcomings. Over time, this erodes trust between lay clients and the professionals.

## Moving forward

The President of the Family Division, Sir Andrew McFarlane, has publicly recognised the urgent need for reform and has emphasised the importance of embedding best practice across the family justice system. In early 2025, the Family Justice Council published "Guidance on Neurodiversity in the Family Justice System for Practitioners". This document represents nearly two years of collaborative work and is the first national attempt to set out clear expectations for practice. It highlights that understanding individual needs and making appropriate adjustments can significantly improve participation and ensure that justice is both fair and effective (Family Justice Council, 2025).

Family Law and Neurodivergence Committee (FLANC) has created practical resources to support both practitioners and families. These include an updated "All About Me" profile as well as toolkits and guidance. FLANC has also collaborated with Family Law in Partnership to design resources for use in non-court dispute resolution settings, ensuring that awareness of neurodivergence is embedded not only in court but also in NCDR.

These developments mark a significant cultural shift. They demonstrate a growing recognition that the needs of neurodivergent individuals cannot be left to chance or to the discretion of individual professionals but must instead be integrated into everyday practice. This book seeks to contribute to that movement by drawing together research, policy, case law, and personal experience into a coordinated and accessible framework for practitioners.

West Midlands ADASS (2024) *Autism and Parental Blame: Blamed Instead of Helped.* WM-ADASS. Available at: https://www.wm-adass.org.uk/improvement/exploring-perspectives-on-autism/parents-perspectives-research-findings

# CHAPTER NINE

# REPRESENTING A NEURODIVERGENT CLIENT

This chapter provides a step-by-step guide for practitioners representing neurodivergent clients within the family justice system. Drawing on the Family Justice Council (FJC) *Guidance on Neurodiversity in the Family Justice System for Practitioners* (2025) and the *Equal Treatment Bench Book* (Judicial College, May 2025 update), the chapter sets out a coherent framework for identifying barriers to effective participation and responding to them through proportionate reasonable adjustments. It explains how the identification of such barriers informs decisions about whether further measures are required, including the appointment of intermediaries in accordance with recent case law or the commissioning of cognitive assessments. In addition, the chapter considers *The Advocate's Gateway* (TAG) toolkits as a practical resource to support this process and to promote fair and meaningful participation in practice.

**Practical realities**

Involvement in family proceedings often coincides with one of the most distressing periods in an individual's life. Navigating the court process can be stressful, emotionally challenging, and overwhelming. Parties may face uncertainty about outcomes, the need to relive traumatic events whilst interacting with unfamiliar professionals, processes, and environments. For neurodivergent adults and children, these challenges are exacerbated and more difficult to manage.

Practitioners often work under significant time pressures and practical constraints. In some cases, instructions are received shortly before an urgent hearing, leaving little opportunity to gather key information about a client's needs. The Family Justice Council guidance provides a structured framework to support the identification of neurodivergence and the implementation of appropriate adjustments.

Although diagnostic recognition of neurodivergence has increased, long waiting times persist. Many individuals involved in family proceedings may not obtain a formal diagnosis whilst involved in the court process. The absence of a diagnostic label does not diminish an individual's needs. Appropriate adjustments and support may still be essential. Practitioners should avoid reliance on diagnostic labels and adopt robust functional approaches to identify and respond to participation needs.

## The 2025 landscape

The Family Justice Council's guidance provides a structured framework for identifying and meeting the needs of neurodivergent participants. It requires early identification of neurodivergence, careful mapping of barriers, and the creation of individualised reasonable adjustments across four domains: (i) outside court, (ii) at court, (iii) during hearings, and (iv) when giving evidence (Family Justice Council, 2025).

Although the *Equal Treatment Bench Book* is primarily directed at the judiciary, it also serves as an invaluable and informative resource for practitioners, offering insight into judicial expectations, case management approaches, and the practical application of reasonable adjustments to support effective participation (Judicial College, 2025). When taken together, these two authorities form a coherent, evidence-based framework ensuring that neurodivergent individuals can participate effectively.

## From guidance to practice: The six-step framework

The Family Justice Council's Guidance provides a clear six-step framework that practitioners should follow (Family Justice Council, 2025). This framework enables practitioners to operationalise equality duties within case preparation and management. It provides a step-by-step approach beginning with early identification and ending with review and monitoring. Each stage ensures that the values of inclusion, accessibility, and procedural fairness are embedded in practice rather than remaining abstract principles. Before looking at each stage in more depth, the six-step framework is summarised below:

| Step | Action | Outcome |
|---|---|---|
| 1 | Identify potential indicators of neurodivergence | Awareness of possible support needs |
| 2 | Assess functional profile and gather information | Understanding how neurodivergence affects participation |
| 3 | Identify barriers to participation | Mapping of procedural and environmental obstacles |
| 4 | Determine reasonable adjustments | Development of tailored strategies to mitigate disadvantage |
| 5 | Apply for reasonable adjustments | Formal integration into case management and directions |
| 6 | Review and monitor | Continuous responsiveness to evolving needs |

### Stage 1: Looking out for neurodivergence

Early identification is essential. Practitioners should consider possible neurodivergence from the first meeting or conversation. The most straightforward starting point is to ask whether the client has a confirmed diagnosis, has received learning or communication support, or believes that neurodivergence may be present.

Where a diagnosis exists, practitioners should consider requesting consent to review relevant reports. This may assist with ascertaining how a client's neurodivergence affects them and may shed light as to what reasonable adjustments are needed. Alternatively, the client may be reluctant to share their assessment report. This could be for various reasons such as the perceived stigma or even still processing the diagnosis. In such circumstances, it would be worth asking the client to detail what reasonable adjustments they think would help them. Where no diagnosis is present, but indicators suggest neurodivergence may be present, practitioners should still proceed using functional screening tools.

TAG Toolkit 10 (*Identifying Vulnerable Witnesses*, 2019, para. 2.2) provides a useful checklist for identifying potential vulnerability. Questions should be tailored to the individual's age, context, and level of understanding, and framed to promote trust and disclosure. A key resource to aid with obtaining such information is the Family Law Advice for the Neurodivergent Community (FLANC) "All About Me" document (FLANC, 2025).

| What may arise | Tips, strategies, and examples of practice |
|---|---|
| Client has confirmed diagnosis of neurodivergence | Request client's consent to review assessments<br>Reports<br>Provide FLANC's "All About Me" form to the client |
| Client suspected to be neurodivergent but undiagnosed | Provide FLANC's "All About Me" form as screening tool; use responses to identify early any potential barriers and to inform adjustments |
| Client anxious about disclosure | Explain that form is for their benefit and shared only with consent to support fair participation |
| Client appears withdrawn, anxious, or struggles to process questions | Use plain, concrete language; allow pauses and reassurance; explain the purpose of questions clearly |
| Client discloses prior educational support or prior assessment | Request consent to obtain relevant reports or contact previous professionals |
| No diagnosis but indicators present (e.g., communication difficulty, sensory sensitivity) | Conduct functional screening using TAG Toolkit 10; make provisional adjustments without delay |
| Client resists the label of neurodivergence | Focus on needs, not terminology; explain that adjustments are about fairness and inclusion, not medicalisation |

## FLANC "All About Me" document

The "All About Me" document, developed by FLANC is a structured self-report form designed for individuals involved in family proceedings who are neurodivergent or who may be neurodivergent (FLANC, 2025). It enables parties to communicate their communication preferences, sensory profile, triggers, strengths, and support needs. The document should be provided to clients as soon as possible.

The document functions as an identification tool, assisting practitioners in recognising potential indicators of neurodivergence even in the absence of formal diagnosis. It also functions as a practical advocacy instrument which can be shared with professionals and the court to ensure the client's bespoke neurodivergent needs/profile is understood.

The document invites individuals to provide information across five main sections:

1. **About me**

    - Preferred name
    - Pronouns
    - Details of any known diagnoses/neurodivergence or suspected neurodivergence
    - A short description of how any diagnosis and/or suspected neurodivergence affects daily communication, concentration, or participation in proceedings

**2. Communication**

- How others should communicate with the individual, what methods are most effective (e.g. written, visual or verbal)
- Common misunderstandings
- How the individual best expresses themselves

**3. Sensory profile**

- Identification of sensory preferences and sensitivities (e.g. light, noise, textures or proximity)
- Details of any self-regulation, coping strategies and sensory aids used

**4. Help at court and in meetings**

- Client's preferences for meeting formats, information delivery, scheduling, and environmental adjustments (e.g. breaks, quieter rooms, or reduced lighting)

**5. Other things to know**

- Information about the individual's strengths, special interests, or personal triggers
- Any other contextual details that may assist professionals in supporting participation

### Benefits for the client

The "All About Me" document empowers clients to articulate their needs in their own words and to have those needs recognised from the outset of proceedings. It reduces the need for repetitive disclosures, mitigates misunderstanding, and allows individuals to be understood as whole people rather than solely through diagnostic labels. The process of completing the form itself can promote self-advocacy and engagement, giving clients a sense of autonomy in proceedings that may otherwise feel overwhelming.

### Benefits for practitioners and the court

For practitioners, the "All About Me" form serves as a concise and consistent reference point summarising the client's functional profile, communication style, and sensory considerations. It supports early planning of reasonable adjustments and enables information to be shared efficiently with all professionals involved, including solicitors, barristers, experts, social workers and court staff. Its structured format facilitates clear and consistent advocacy for adjustments, providing documentary evidence of the client's expressed needs and preferences.

For the court, receipt of a completed form promotes procedural fairness and transparency by ensuring that judicial and administrative personnel are aware of any relevant barriers and the reasonable adjustments proposed to address them.

### Stage 2: Assessing functional profile and gathering additional information if required

Understanding the individual's functional profile is critical to identifying appropriate adjustments. Practitioners should gather information about the client's cognitive, sensory, and emotional needs, as well as preferred communication formats. This may include reviewing reports from psychologists, speech and language therapists, or educational professionals, or requesting an intermediary assessment where appropriate (Family Justice Council, 2025).

Becoming aware that a client may be neurodivergent will inevitably prompt the need for further information. Practitioners should, with appropriate consent, obtain relevant information from health, education, or social care professionals, family members or friends. Where necessary, a formal neurodevelopmental and/or intermediary assessment may be required to determine communication and accessibility requirements during proceedings (Family Justice Council, 2025).

| **What may arise** | **Tips, strategies, and examples of practice** |
|---|---|
| Limited or outdated documentation | Use the “All About Me” form as current summary; request updated reports if necessary |
| Neurodivergence suspected but not confirmed | Note observed indicators such as communication style or sensory responses; seek consent to gather background information and consider referral for assessment |
| Existing diagnosis but limited supporting information | Request recent reports from professionals or insights from family and/or friends to understand the functional and communication needs |
| Unclear communication or processing needs | Consult President’s Practice Guidance (2025) and TAG Toolkit 14 when considering whether an intermediary assessment is needed. Use plain language, visual aids, or written prompts to support understanding |
| Sensory sensitivities affecting participation | Adjust the environment (e.g., quieter space, reduced lighting, regular breaks) and record accommodations in the functional profile. |

### Stage 3: Identifying barriers to participation

Barriers may arise from communication demands, sensory triggers, or procedural complexity. Practitioners should systematically map these across four domains: outside court, at court, during hearings, and when giving evidence (Family Justice Council, 2025).

| What may arise | Tips, strategies, and examples of practice |
|---|---|
| Barriers engaging with professionals away from court | Provide information in accessible formats (e.g., visual summaries, plain language), offer consistent points of contact and flexibility with appointments |
| Barriers attending or navigating the court environment | Arrange pre-hearing visits, provide visual courtroom guides, identify quiet waiting areas and sensory adjustments where needed |
| Barriers participating in court proceedings but not giving evidence | Use intermediaries or advocates to support communication, ensure clear explanations of roles and processes are given and allow for additional processing time |
| Barriers when giving evidence | Use breaks, simplified questioning, consider fidget toys or adapting the method in which evidence is given |

### Stage 4: Reasonable adjustments

Adjustments must be tailored to the individual's needs. The Family Justice Council guidance identifies that adjustments fall into three areas: communication, environment, and structure/timing. Moreover, they should be considered across four scenarios. These scenarios include when away from court, while at court, during a hearing, and when giving evidence. Once participation barriers have been identified, proposed adjustments must be considered with the client. This ensures they are practical, proportionate, and appropriate. The court's agreement to endorse and implement any adjustments will always be required (Family Justice Council, 2025).

| What may arise | Tips, strategies, and examples of practice |
|---|---|
| Barriers to effective communication | Use preferred contact methods (e.g., email); keep language concrete and concise; avoid figurative terms; build in pauses and check understanding. |
| Sensory or environmental discomfort | Modify lighting or noise levels; permit movement or use of sensory aids; identify a quiet, private waiting space; offer advance familiarisation with settings. |
| Difficulty managing time, transitions, or unpredictability | Provide visual or written schedules; give notice of changes; plan sessions at times that suit concentration; include regular breaks. |
| Need to coordinate and monitor adjustments | Match adjustments to each stage of the process; work collaboratively with the individual; document agreements clearly; revisit and refine as needed. |

### Stage 5: Seeking reasonable adjustments

There is no set form for requesting reasonable adjustments, but HMCTS guidance explains what may be provided and how to arrange it. Requests should outline the individual's needs, how these affect participation, and what measures are required to ensure fair engagement in the process.

### Stage 6: Reviewing and monitoring reasonable adjustments during proceedings

Adjustments should be identified and arranged as early as possible, ideally before or at the start of proceedings. They must be reviewed throughout the case to ensure they remain appropriate and specifically reconsidered at a ground-rules hearing before any evidence is given, in line with paragraph 5 of PD3AA.

### Intermediaries

This subsection builds upon stages 2 to 5 of the six-stage framework and focuses specifically on the role of intermediaries within the family justice system. It should be read as part of the wider process of identifying barriers, determining whether reasonable adjustments can secure effective participation, and deciding whether additional procedural safeguards are required.

Practitioners should also be aware of the *Practice Guidance by the President of the Family Division on the use of intermediaries, lay advocates and cognitive assessments in the Family Court*, which provides authoritative direction on when and how such measures may be considered within the process (Judiciary of England and Wales, 2025).

### Distinguishing participation from giving evidence as separate concepts

Part 3A of the Family Procedure Rules 2010 draws an important distinction between a party's ability to participate in proceedings and their ability to give evidence. Although these concepts are often treated as interchangeable in practice, they engage fundamentally different cognitive, emotional, and neurological demands. This distinction is particularly significant for neurodivergent individuals.

Participation in proceedings refers to a person's capacity to understand, engage with, and be involved in the legal process as a whole. It encompasses the ability to comprehend the issues in dispute, communicate with legal representatives, provide instructions, read and process documentation, attend hearings, and make informed decisions about the case. For many neurodivergent individuals, effective participation is achievable where appropriate reasonable adjustments are in place, such as additional time, written communication, predictable structure, or remote attendance.

By contrast, giving evidence is a discrete and highly demanding forensic task. It typically involves answering questions orally, often under cross-examination, in a fast-paced and adversarial environment. This process places significant strain on working memory, language processing, emotional regulation, and sensory tolerance. Neurodivergent individuals may experience heightened vulnerability in this context, including cognitive overload, shutdown, dissociation, loss of speech, or impaired recall under pressure. These reactions do not reflect a lack of understanding or credibility, but rather the incompatibility of traditional evidential methods with certain neurocognitive profiles.

Crucially, a neurodivergent individual may be fully capable of participating meaningfully in proceedings while being unable to give evidence safely, reliably, or fairly. Part 3A recognises that vulnerability is context-specific and task-dependent, and that fairness requires the court to assess participation and evidence-giving separately. Failure to maintain this distinction risks excluding neurodivergent individuals from effective access to justice or placing undue weight on evidence obtained in circumstances that undermine reliability.

The assessment of whether an intermediary is required must be undertaken on a task-specific and hearing-specific basis. It should be firmly grounded in the individual's functional profile as identified at stage 2, and in the specific barriers mapped at stage 3 of the six-stage framework. Practitioners should avoid blanket approaches and instead ensure that any application to the court for the appointment of an intermediary is fully particularised.

## The legal framework for intermediary involvement

Intermediaries operate entirely within the framework created by Part 3A of the Family Procedure Rules 2010 and Practice Direction 3AA. The court is under a proactive duty to consider whether any party or witness is vulnerable and whether that vulnerability is likely to affect their ability to participate in proceedings or give evidence.

The purpose of Part 3A is to achieve a fair hearing by ensuring that participation and the quality of evidence is not diminished by vulnerability. This duty applies regardless of whether a formal diagnosis exists or not.

Where a party or witness is identified as vulnerable and their participation or evidence is likely to be affected, the court must consider whether it is necessary to make participation directions under r.3A.6. This may include the use of an intermediary to support participation in proceedings under r.3A.8(1)(d) or to assist a party or witness when giving evidence under r.3A.8(1)(e).

## The test for the appointment of an intermediary

In *Re M (A Child: Intermediaries)* [2025] EWCA Civ 440, the Court of Appeal clarified the correct approach to the appointment of intermediaries in family proceedings. The Court confirmed that the sole test is whether the appointment of an intermediary is necessary to secure a fair hearing, whether for the proceedings as a whole or for a particular task or hearing. This represents a clear rejection of any alternative or heightened test previously suggested in earlier High Court authority.

The Court further held that intermediaries are not expert witnesses and do not fall within Part 25 of the Family Procedure Rules. Applications for intermediary assistance must therefore be made under Part 18, within the participation framework established by Part 3A and Practice Direction 3AA. Decisions concerning intermediary involvement must be person-specific, and task-specific, and grounded in a structured assessment of the individual's ability to participate effectively.

The judgment places particular emphasis on early identification of vulnerability and effective case management, making clear that intermediary assistance should not be approached on a blanket basis. Any proposal for intermediary involvement must be supported by adequate evidence, and the court must consider what can reasonably be expected of advocates before concluding that intermediary assistance is necessary. Importantly, the court is required to give clear, recorded reasons for granting or refusing any directions relating to intermediary support.

The Court of Appeal also confirmed that intermediary assistance may, where necessary, extend beyond the courtroom to include conferences and meetings outside the hearing itself. Such assistance is not automatic and requires separate judicial consideration, reinforcing the need for a careful, proportionate, and task-specific approach.

In determining whether intermediary assistance is necessary, the court must have regard to the mandatory checklist set out in Rule 3A.7, which includes consideration of the individual's mental disorder or impairment, any physical disability, age and maturity, level of understanding, communication needs, social and cultural background, the nature and complexity of the proceedings, and the availability and proportionality of participation measures. Practitioners should ensure that evidence and submissions are mapped directly against these factors, focusing on functional impact and participation barriers, rather than relying solely on diagnostic labels.

### Rule 3A.7 mandatory checklist

When the court is considering whether an intermediary is necessary it must have regard to the mandatory checklist contained within Rule 3A.7. This checklist covers the following:

- Mental disorder or impairment
- Physical disability
- Age and maturity
- Level of understanding
- Communication needs
- Social and cultural background
- Nature and complexity of the proceedings
- Availability and cost of measures

Practitioners should ensure that evidence and submissions are tailored to address the checklist.

### When skilled advocacy may remove the need for an intermediary

The 2025 guidance places strong emphasis on the role of skilled advocacy before an intermediary is considered. Advocates are expected to embed neurodiversity-informed communication into everyday practice.

This includes the techniques set out across *The Advocate's Gateway toolkits,* in particular:

- Toolkit 1: General principles from research practice and guidance

- Toolkit 3: Planning to question a vulnerable witness
- Toolkit 4: Questioning vulnerable witnesses including children and adults
- Toolkit 5: Planning to question someone with 'hidden' disabilities: specific language impairment, dyslexia, dyspraxia, dyscalculia and ADHD
- Toolkit 10: Identifying vulnerable witnesses
- Toolkit 14: Using intermediaries and other specialist communication support

The table below illustrates how neurodivergence-informed advocacy practices, as set out in the Advocate's Gateway toolkits, can be applied in practice to support effective participation in court without reliance on intermediary appointment.

| **Adjustment / practice** | **Advocate's Gateway Toolkit (neurodivergence-relevant)** | **Neurodivergent communication need addressed** | **Example of how the advocate applies this in practice** | **Why skilled advocacy may be sufficient (without an intermediary)** |
|---|---|---|---|---|
| Use of plain, concrete, and literal language | Toolkits on questioning vulnerable witnesses; autism and communication difference guidance | Difficulty processing abstract, inferred, or implied meaning | "Did you arrive at the house before 6pm?" rather than "Were you there early?" | Removes linguistic ambiguity and reduces misinterpretation, enabling accurate understanding and response |
| Structured, sequenced questioning | Toolkits on effective questioning and managing evidence | Executive functioning differences; difficulty organising information | "I will ask you about the morning first, then the afternoon, then the evening." | Predictable structure supports coherence and focus without the need for specialist facilitation |

| | | | | |
|---|---|---|---|---|
| Slower pace and increased processing time | Toolkits on communication needs and effective participation | Delayed processing or response time | Advocate asks a question and allows silence before rephrasing or moving on | Adequate processing time enables meaningful participation without communication breakdown |
| Avoidance of abstract, figurative, or hypothetical language | Toolkits addressing autism and neurodivergent communication styles | Literal interpretation of language | Avoids metaphors such as "breaking point" and asks concrete questions instead | Ensures questions are interpreted as intended, maintaining evidential reliability |
| Clear signposting of topic or temporal changes | Toolkits on structuring examinations | Difficulty with contextual or temporal switching | "I am now going to ask you about what happened the following day, Tuesday." | Explicit transitions support orientation and reduce confusion during questioning |
| One concept per question; avoidance of compound questions | Toolkits on avoiding complex or leading questions | Difficulty holding multiple concepts in working memory | Separates "Did you see him?" and "What did he say?" into two questions | Reduces cognitive load and supports accurate, reliable responses |
| Use of written or visual supports (where appropriate) | Toolkits on practical courtroom adaptations | Strength in visual processing; difficulty with auditory-only information | Refers to a written timeline or document while asking questions | Visual reinforcement supports comprehension without specialist intervention |
| Regular, explicit checks of understanding | Toolkits on monitoring comprehension | Masking, acquiescence, or delayed recognition of misunderstanding | "Can you tell me what you understand my question to be asking?" | Identifies misunderstanding early while preserving procedural fairness |
| Predictable questioning style and courtroom structure | Toolkits on managing anxiety and participation | Anxiety arising from unpredictability | "I will ask five questions on this topic and then stop." | Predictability reduces anxiety that might otherwise impair participation |

| Proportionate adaptation to sensory sensitivities (where relevant) | Toolkits on environmental and procedural adjustments | Sensory overload affecting concentration or regulation | Requests short breaks or minimises unnecessary courtroom movement | Environmental adjustments can secure effective participation without intermediary support |
|---|---|---|---|---|

Where these measures are sufficient to secure fair participation the appointment of an intermediary is unlikely to be necessary. Advocates must therefore be able to explain why these professional skills would not suffice before seeking intermediary appointment.

## The role and limits of advocates

Advocates bear responsibility for identifying vulnerability, adapting their communication style, and making submissions as to the measures required to ensure a fair hearing. However, advocates are not themselves the special measure. Lawyers are not trained intermediaries and cannot safely assume responsibility for ongoing monitoring of comprehension, real-time processing support, dynamic adjustment of communication, or sensory and emotional regulation.

These functions fall outside the professional competence of advocates and cannot be substituted by skilled advocacy alone. Where advocates reach the limits of what professional adaptation can achieve, intermediary involvement must be properly considered.

## Narrowing the scope of intermediary involvement

Where intermediary assistance is directed, the court should define the scope of the role narrowly and proportionately. Directions should specify which hearing or stage the intermediary will attend, whether assistance relates to participation, evidence-giving, or both, and whether support is required in conferences or legal meetings. Over-broad or undefined directions risk undermining proportionality, effective case management, and the appropriate use of limited resources.

### Continuity of intermediary support

Different intermediaries may attend different hearings, requiring the vulnerable party to repeatedly explain their needs. This repetition has the potential to undermine the trust, rapport, and emotional safety that may already have been established. Where possible, practitioners should therefore seek continuity of intermediary support.

### Creative models of participation

Intermediary support is not limited to traditional, in-court questioning. In C (Children: Welfare) (No.2) [2020] EWFC B36, the court recognised that tailored participation may include giving evidence through typed responses. Other adjustments may include visual sequencing of questions, written prompts, modified courtroom layouts, staged questioning, permission to use a fidget item, and the provision of additional breaks. When properly implemented, these measures enhance communication without changing the substance of the evidence, ensuring participation is enabled rather than reconfigured.

### Cognitive assessments and Part 25

A cognitive assessment is expert evidence and is governed by Part 25 of the Family Procedure Rules. The instruction of an expert to conduct a cognitive assessment will only be granted if it is necessary to resolve the proceedings justly, pursuant to FPR r 25.4(3).

This subsection is distinct from intermediary provision. Cognitive assessments perform an evidential function and must not be conflated with the facilitative role of intermediaries under Part 3A of the Family

Procedure Rules. The purpose of a cognitive assessment is to assist the court by providing evidence of functional cognitive impact. It does not determine whether special measures should be granted and does not of itself justify the appointment of an intermediary.

A cognitive assessment may be necessary where there is uncertainty about a party's cognitive functioning, where processing speed, memory, attention, or comprehension are in question, where there is disagreement about the level of vulnerability, or where the court requires evidence of functional impact.

Where a cognitive assessment is relied upon to support the use of an intermediary, it must provide evidence that the use of an intermediary is necessary to enable the party to participate in the proceedings fairly. It must also provide reasons, supported by evidence, explaining why fair participation could not be achieved by alternative means.

In addressing those questions, the assessment must consider the party's participation at case management hearings, conferences, the taking of instructions, and the giving of evidence at a contested hearing.

A cognitive assessment that fails to address participation in a stage-specific and task-specific manner will be of limited assistance to the court when determining whether intermediary involvement is necessary.

### The relationship between cognitive assessments and intermediary assessments

Cognitive assessments and intermediary involvement serve distinct but complementary purposes. Cognitive assessments provide expert evidence about functional capacity, including processing speed, working memory, language comprehension, executive functioning, attentional regulation, and tolerance of stress. Intermediaries, by contrast, provide real-time facilitative support to enable effective participation and/or the giving of evidence.

A cognitive assessment does not determine whether an intermediary will be appointed. That decision is judicial, governed by Part 3A and Practice Direction 3AA. The relationship between cognitive assessment and intermediary involvement is therefore evidential rather than determinative. In every case, the key question remains whether intermediary involvement is necessary to secure a fair hearing.

This table summarises the key differences and points of overlap between cognitive assessments and intermediary involvement.

| Feature | Intermediaries | Cognitive Assessments |
|---|---|---|
| Legal basis | Part 3A FPR and Practice Direction 3AA | Part 25 FPR |
| Nature | Facilitative measure | Expert evidence |
| Purpose | Facilitate participation and evidence-giving | Provide evidence of functional cognitive impact |
| Evidential status | Not expert evidence | Expert evidence |
| Determines appointment | No | No |
| Role in proceedings | Real-time communication and processing support | Informs judicial decision-making |
| Scope | Hearing-specific and task-specific | Broad functional assessment |
| Relationship | May be informed by cognitive assessment | May support application for intermediary involvement |

## Practical checklist for practitioners

### Stage 1: Identification of neurodivergence

- ☐ Consider possible neurodivergence from the first point of contact
- ☐ Ask about diagnosis, suspected neurodivergence, and prior educational or communication support
- ☐ Avoid reliance on diagnostic labels and focus on functional impact
- ☐ Use TAG Toolkit 10 to screen for vulnerability
- ☐ Provide the FLANC All About Me document at an early stage
- ☐ Explain the purpose of information gathering and obtain informed consent for any disclosure

### Stage 2: Functional profile and information gathering

- ☐ Identify communication preferences, sensory sensitivities, processing needs, and emotional regulation issues
- ☐ Review existing reports where available and up-to-date
- ☐ Seek consent to obtain further information from professionals or family where appropriate
- ☐ Record observations about processing speed, comprehension, and regulation

- ☐ Consider whether further assessment may be required and on what evidential basis

**Stage 3: Identifying barriers to participation**

- ☐ Map barriers across the four domains outside court, at court, during hearings, and when giving evidence
- ☐ Distinguish clearly between participation in proceedings and the task of giving evidence
- ☐ Identify whether barriers are task specific or hearing specific
- ☐ Record barriers in functional rather than diagnostic terms

**Stage 4: Reasonable adjustments**

- ☐ Consider communication, environment, and structure or timing adjustments
- ☐ Discuss proposed adjustments with the client and confirm they are appropriate and proportionate
- ☐ Consider whether skilled advocacy and courtroom adjustments are sufficient
- ☐ Ensure proposed adjustments are linked directly to identified barriers

## Stage 5: Seeking reasonable adjustments and participation directions

- ☐ Make timely applications for reasonable adjustments or participation directions
- ☐ Clearly explain functional impact and why adjustments are required
- ☐ Where intermediary involvement is sought, explain why skilled advocacy alone cannot secure fairness
- ☐ Ensure applications are task specific and hearing specific

### Intermediaries

- ☐ Apply the sole test of necessity to secure a fair hearing in line with Re M
- ☐ Distinguish participation from evidence-giving
- ☐ Map evidence and submissions to the Rule 3A.7 mandatory checklist
- ☐ Consider what can reasonably be expected of advocates using The Advocate's Gateway toolkits
- ☐ If intermediary involvement is directed, seek clear and proportionate directions defining scope and stage
- ☐ Consider continuity of intermediary support where possible

## Skilled advocacy

☐ Apply neurodivergence informed advocacy techniques as standard practice

☐ Be familiar with relevant Advocate's Gateway toolkits, particularly Toolkits 1, 3, 4, 5, 10, and 14

☐ Use plain, concrete language and structured questioning

☐ Allow adequate processing time and check understanding explicitly

☐ Recognise and respect the limits of advocacy

## Cognitive assessments and Part 25

☐ Consider whether a cognitive assessment is necessary to resolve the proceedings justly

☐ Ensure any Part 25 application satisfies the necessity test under r 25.4(3)

☐ If relied upon to support intermediary involvement, ensure the assessment addresses

- why an intermediary is necessary
- why alternative measures cannot secure fairness
- participation at each stage of proceedings

☐ Treat cognitive assessments as evidential not determinative

### Stage 6: Review and monitoring

☐ Review adjustments regularly throughout proceedings

☐ Revisit participation needs at each key hearing

☐ Ensure ground rules hearings are properly used before evidence is given

☐ Remain responsive to changes in the client's needs or presentation

### References

Family Justice Council (2025) *Guidance on Neurodiversity in the Family Justice System for Practitioners*. London: Judiciary of England and Wales.

Family Law Accommodation Network (2025) *All About Me – Client Information Form*. London: FLANC. Available at: https://flanc.org.uk/wp-content/uploads/2025/01/FLANC-All-About-Me-document.pdf

Judicial College (2025) *Equal Treatment Bench Book*. May 2025 update. London: Judicial College.

National Autistic Society (2015) *The SPELL Framework*. London: NAS.

Judiciary of England and Wales (2025) *Practice Guidance by the President of the Family Division: The use of intermediaries, lay advocates and cognitive assessments in the Family Court*. Available at: https://www.judiciary.uk/guidance-and-resources/practice-guidance-by-the-pfd-the-use-of-intermediaries-lay-advocates-and-cognitive-assessments-in-the-family-court/

The Advocate's Gateway (2019) *Toolkit 10: Identifying Vulnerable Witnesses*. London: The Advocate's Gateway.

The Advocate's Gateway (2019) *Toolkit 14: Ground Rules Hearings and the Fair Treatment of Vulnerable People*. London: The Advocate's Gateway.

# CHAPTER TEN

# NEURODIVERGENCE IN PUBLIC LAW PROCEEDINGS

## Introduction

Neurodivergence is an increasingly significant factor in public law children proceedings in England and Wales. As established in previous chapters, neurodivergent conditions reflect cognitive variation. These variations are differences, not deficits. Neurodivergence does not imply or equate to diminished parental capacity.

When neurodivergent needs are not recognised, understood, or accommodated, both parents and children face potential systemic disadvantage. Failing to identify and understand someone's neurodivergent profile can distort professional assessments, limit meaningful participation, and lead to outcomes that are neither fair nor lawful. Parents may be misjudged through a lens of deficit rather than difference, while children's behaviours risk being misunderstood or pathologised, often resulting in inappropriate interventions.

Research by Professor Rob George and colleagues at University College London (UCL) has demonstrated that autistic adults frequently encounter profound barriers within the family courts (George, Crane and Remington, 2020). These include misinterpretations of communication style, sensory overload arising from court environments, and a lack of appropriate adjustments. Such obstacles not only impede access to justice but also raise significant concerns regarding compliance with Articles 6 and 8 of the European Convention on Human Rights (ECHR).

This chapter considers the statutory and procedural framework that governs neurodivergence in public law proceedings. It explores what local authorities are required to do and the importance of specialist assessments. It also considers the crucial distinction between trauma and neurodevelopmental needs. Drawing upon UCL's research, relevant case law, and emerging practice tools such as the Model for Assessing Learning Difficulties and Vulnerabilities (MALD®), this chapter proposes an integrated approach based on equality, inclusion and fairness.

## The legal framework

The Children Act 1989 imposes several core duties:

**Section 17:** Requires local authorities to safeguard and promote the welfare of children in need, including disabled children, a category that frequently encompasses neurodivergence.

**Section 20:** Allows children to be accommodated with parental consent. Where parents are neurodivergent, such consent must be informed and accessible.

In practice, "consent" under section 20 requires more than a signature or apparent agreement. For neurodivergent parents, informed agreement may require information to be provided in accessible formats, additional time to process, and an active check of understanding (including what section 20 does and does not mean, what alternatives exist, and how the arrangement can be ended). The professional task is to ensure the parent can make and communicate a decision, not merely to record compliance. Clear written summaries, predictable follow-up, and careful recording of steps taken to support understanding will reduce the risk of later dispute about whether agreement was real, informed, and fairly obtained.

**Section 34:** Imposes a duty to promote reasonable contact between children and parents, requiring adaptation to meet sensory, communication and processing needs.

**Section 47:** Mandates child protection investigations. Professionals must avoid mistaking atypical communication or behaviour for evidence of neglect or abuse.

### The Care Act 2014

The Care Act imposes duties on adult services to assess and support needs where a parent's neurodivergence impacts their daily functioning.

### The Equality Act 2010

Neurodivergence typically meets the Act's definition of "disability," triggering duties to avoid discrimination and make reasonable adjustments. The Public Sector Equality Duty (PSED) requires local authorities to:

- Eliminate discrimination and harassment
- Advance equality of opportunity
- Foster understanding between neurodivergent and non-neurodivergent individuals

These duties require proactive identification of neurodivergence and anticipatory planning to ensure accessibility at every stage of proceedings (Family Justice Council, 2025).

### Duties towards neurodivergent parents

These statutory duties intersect with the court's obligation to secure effective participation and procedural fairness.

The court's fundamental obligation is to ensure a fair hearing under Article 6 ECHR. Fairness requires that each party can effectively participate in proceedings and present their case. For neurodivergent parents, this includes the right to adjustments that address barriers created by communication, sensory or processing differences (Family Justice Council, 2025).

Participation is not limited to giving evidence at a final hearing. Part 3A and Practice Direction 3AA require the court to identify vulnerability and consider whether participation directions are needed so that the party can engage throughout the case, including conferences, assessments, statement preparation, hearings, and decision-making. For neurodivergent parents, effective participation may depend on practical measures such as structured communication, written summaries, predictable scheduling, adjusted questioning style, and support to manage cognitive load. Practitioners should therefore address participation needs as a case-management issue early, rather than treating adjustments as an "add-on" once a hearing is listed.

All public bodies involved in care proceedings, including local authorities, CAFCASS and the judiciary, are subject to the PSED under section 149 of the Equality Act 2010. This requires active consideration of how policies and practices affect neurodivergent individuals and the implementation of reasonable adjustments to ensure equitable participation.

## Procedural roadmap: where neurodivergence matters in public law proceedings

### Timetabling and early action

Public law proceedings operate under intense time pressure, and delay can quickly harden narratives about "non-engagement," "lack of insight," or "failure to change." Where neurodivergence is relevant, adjustments and specialist input need to be front-loaded. If screening, participation measures, or specialist assessments are left until late in proceedings, the parent may be judged against neurotypical expectations without the supports required to demonstrate their true capacity. Early identification, clear instructions to professionals, and predictable case planning protect fairness and improve the reliability of evidence used to make life-changing decisions.

## Neurodivergence across the lifecycle of public law proceedings

Neurodivergence can shape a case from the pre-proceedings stage. It may affect how parents engage with PLO letters, meetings, and safety plans. It can influence how written expectations are understood and followed. It may also affect how professionals interpret missed appointments, delay, or apparent inconsistency.

Once proceedings are issued, neurodivergence is relevant at gatekeeping and the CMH. Participation directions and the need for specialist assessment should be identified early.

Neurodivergence can affect the reliability of evidence. This includes parenting assessments, contact observations, and professional interviews. Difficulties are more likely where cognitive load and sensory demands are high.

By the IRH and final hearing, there is a risk that neurotypical expectations become embedded in the case narrative. This is more likely if reasonable adjustments and functional formulation are not addressed. Neurodivergence remains relevant after final orders. It affects placement support, contact arrangements, and the sustainability of the care plan.

## Recognising and understanding neurodivergence

A significant challenge arises where neurodivergence is not recognised or is misinterpreted. Many parents involved in care proceedings have undiagnosed or undisclosed neurodivergent traits. Early signs may include difficulty processing information, sensitivity to sensory stimuli, apparent disorganisation, or atypical communication patterns.

Professionals must be alert to behaviours that might be indicative of neurodivergence, such as:

- Struggling to maintain eye contact or appearing emotionally detached
- Difficulty following complex instructions or deadlines
- Overwhelm or shutdown in meetings or hearings
- Literal or blunt responses to questions
- Inconsistent engagement with proceedings and/or professionals

These traits are often mistaken as defiance, avoidance or lack of insight. In reality, they may reflect anxiety, processing delay or sensory overload (George, Crane and Remington 2020). The professional duty is therefore one of curiosity and inquiry: to ask why a parent presents in a particular way and what adaptations might help them to engage.

## Duties to neurodivergent children

Alongside duties to parents, local authorities have parallel and distinct duties towards neurodivergent children under the Children Act 1989 and the Equality Act 2010. They must ensure identification, assessment and support are timely and appropriate. Neurodivergent children frequently meet the definition of 'children in need' under section 17 of the Children Act 1989.

## Identification and assessment

Children are sometimes denied assessments for autism or ADHD during proceedings under the mistaken belief that such evaluations must be delayed until permanence decisions are made. This approach risks unsafe outcomes. Research emphasises the importance of distinguishing between trauma and neurodivergence, which frequently co-exist (George, Crane and Remington 2020). Timely neurodevelopmental assessment ensures accurate formulation, guiding placement, contact and care decisions. The Family Justice Council (2025) recommends that local authorities refer early for screening and integrate functional assessments such as occupational therapy and speech and language input.

## Support and services

Under section 17 of the Children Act 1989, neurodivergent children are entitled to tailored services, including Education, Health and Care Plans (EHCPs) under the Children and Families Act 2014. UCL's findings demonstrate that autistic children often experience significant distress in unsuitable environments, necessitating sensory and communication-based support (George, Crane and Remington 2020). Support must therefore be proactive, addressing sensory regulation, executive function, and communication needs.

## How neurodivergence may be misinterpreted

| Behaviour Observed | Common Misinterpretation | Possible Neurodivergent Explanation |
| --- | --- | --- |
| Avoids eye contact | Cold, indifferent, lacking empathy | Eye contact may be uncomfortable or distracting for an autistic person |
| Appears forgetful or misses appointments | Disorganised, non-compliant | Executive functioning differences associated with ADHD or dyspraxia |
| Responds bluntly or literally | Rude, defiant, lacking insight | Literal processing or difficulty with social inference |
| Becomes overwhelmed or tearful | Manipulative or unstable | Sensory or emotional overload, not intentional distress |
| Over-shares or repeats detail | Unfocussed, obsessive | Attempt to self-regulate or maintain control in stressful context |
| Struggles to follow oral questioning | Evasive or inattentive | Processing delay or auditory overload |
| Inconsistent engagement with professionals | Resistant to support | Anxiety around authority or trauma-related avoidance |
| Reluctance to engage with parenting courses | Lacks motivation | Content or format not adapted to learning style or sensory needs and/or struggles with executive dysfunction |

### Threshold language

A particular risk in care proceedings is that neurodivergent presentation is translated into threshold language without a functional analysis. Descriptors such as "non-compliant", "lacking insight", "chaotic", "fails to prioritise", or "emotionally detached" can become proxies for harm when they may instead reflect executive functioning differences, processing delay, sensory overload, or communication style.

Threshold must focus on evidence of impairment attributable to parenting and the impact on the child, not neurodivergent traits themselves. Practitioners should therefore scrutinise how concerns are formulated, require specificity about what has happened, and ensure that any apparent difficulty is assessed in context and with appropriate adjustments before it is relied upon as proof of risk.

### Reasonable adjustments and best practice

The Family Justice Council (2025) guidance provides clear examples of reasonable adjustments:

**Communication adjustments**: Use plain language, written summaries, one question at a time, and provide advance notice.

**Environmental adjustments**: Provide quiet waiting areas, virtual attendance options, and minimise sensory triggers.

**Procedural adjustments**: Shorter hearings with breaks, predictable scheduling, intermediaries or advocates, and visual aids.

**Support adjustments**: Neurodiversity aware parenting programmes, diagnostic screening referrals, and case management plans addressing neurodivergent needs.

These adjustments ensure fairness and accessibility so that parents can demonstrate their true ability.

## Expert evidence and rapid screening

Expert input is crucial in cases involving neurodivergence. Courts must ensure compliance with Family Procedure Rules Part 25, requiring that expert evidence is relevant, proportionate and necessary.

Dr Tom Grange's rapid screening model provides an effective response to diagnostic delays. Screening can indicate whether a full diagnostic assessment is required and recommend immediate adjustments. UCL research confirms that many autistic adults enter proceedings without formal diagnosis; early screening prevents injustice by ensuring interim support is provided promptly (George, Crane and Remington 2020).

## Specialist parenting assessments

In *Re E (A Child) (Care and Placement Orders)* [2023] EWCA Civ 721, the Court of Appeal emphasised the significance of assessing neurodivergence and the specific needs arising from it. In this case, the Court of Appeal allowed a mother's appeal against the making of care and placement orders. This was due to the refusal of a psychological assessment of the mother despite there being concerns that she had autism. At paragraph 35, Lord Justice Baker sets out a three-stage approach when considering placing or leaving a child with parents:

> *"The first stage – identifying the level of support needed by the family – involves a thorough assessment of both parent and child. In most cases, a social work assessment will be sufficient. But in some cases, where the parent and/or the child have or may have other needs, other assessments will be necessary. Where, for example, the parent or child has a physical or learning disability, specialist assessment will normally be required. It is recognised*

> *that the assessment of parents with learning difficulties or disabilities requires specialist understanding and techniques, commonly delivered in this country through the so-called "PAMS" (Parenting Assessment Manual Assessments) model. A parent with autism may or may not have a learning disability, but their neurodiverse condition merits assessment for the same reason – to identify the level of support needed and, importantly, how and by whom it should be delivered. Such an assessment can only be carried out by someone with the requisite expertise".*

Generic parenting assessments are often inappropriate for neurodivergent parents because they are built around neurotypical expectations of communication, organisation and responsiveness. Neurodivergent presentation, especially under stress, can be misread as deficient parenting when it may simply reflect difference. Research indicates autistic parents are frequently misjudged due to atypical communication rather than lack of parenting ability (George, Crane and Remington 2020).

Neurodivergence should be identified and flagged at the earliest stage. A specialist assessment should then be commissioned promptly. This is particularly important where the court must decide whether the parent can provide "good enough" care with appropriate support and adjustments. Failing to distinguish difference from deficit risks discriminatory outcomes and undermines compliance with the Equality Act 2010 and Article 6 ECHR (effective participation and procedural fairness).

Accordingly, practitioners must closely examine both the assessor's competence and the tools used in the parenting assessment. This includes checking what specialist training the assessor has undertaken, how recent and robust it is, who provided it and their credentials, and whether the assessor can apply that learning in practice. Practitioners should also consider whether the proposed model and toolkit are relevant and appropriate to the family's needs, enable proper exploration of the asserted risks in the case, and are delivered in a way the parents can meaningfully understand and process.

## Adverse Childhood Experiences and Trauma

Adverse Childhood Experiences (ACEs) encompass experiences of abuse, neglect, and household dysfunction (Felitti et al., 1998). Exposure to ACEs can have lasting effects on emotional regulation, cognition, and physical health, and they are often considered within a trauma-informed framework in social care and family law proceedings. However, the increasing tendency of professionals to interpret behavioural difficulties solely through a trauma lens can lead to the conflation of trauma with neurodivergence, creating significant risks for accurate assessment and fair decision-making (Family Justice Council, 2025).

Behaviours such as hypervigilance, executive dysfunction, or emotional withdrawal may be interpreted as trauma responses when, in fact, they could also represent features of neurodevelopmental conditions such as autism or ADHD. Similarly, autistic masking, the effort to consciously hide or suppress autistic traits to conform socially, may be mistaken for trauma-related suppression or avoidance. Since trauma and neurodivergence frequently coexist, careful, nuanced assessment is essential to distinguish between the two and to understand how each influences a child or parent's presentation and functioning.

To achieve this, letters of instruction to experts in family proceedings should address:

- a full developmental history
- analysis of the onset and persistence of behaviours
- consideration of masking

- expertise in both neurodevelopment and trauma.

This comprehensive, dual-informed approach ensures that interventions and support plans are appropriately tailored. Trauma-focused therapies, for instance, must be adapted to align with neurodivergent processing styles to be effective. Failure to make these distinctions risks misdiagnosis, inappropriate therapeutic recommendations, unfair attribution of blame to parents, and, in some cases, the unnecessary removal of children from their families.

Understanding the interaction between ACEs and neurodivergence is therefore critical to ensuring assessments and judicial decisions are fair, accurate, and aligned with both safeguarding duties and the positive obligations under Article 8 of the European Convention on Human Rights.

## Conclusion

Ultimately, neurodivergence is not a marker of parental unfitness, but it can profoundly affect how parents and children are assessed and understood within public law proceedings. Fairness requires early identification of functional needs, timely specialist input where necessary, and adjustments that enable meaningful participation throughout the case. Without this, difference can be misread as deficit and embedded in evidence, threshold, and welfare analysis. A neurodiversity-informed approach supports more accurate assessment, more lawful decision-making, and care plans that are genuinely workable for children and families.

## Practical checklist for practitioners

### Early Identification

- ☐ Have potential neurodivergent traits been actively considered, even where there is no formal diagnosis?
- ☐ Have behaviours been explored through a lens of difference rather than deficit?
- ☐ Has neurodivergence been identified and flagged at pre-proceedings, gatekeeping or CMH stage?

### Participation and Fairness

- ☐ Have participation needs been assessed in accordance with FPR Part 3A and Practice Direction 3AA?
- ☐ Are appropriate adjustments in place for meetings, assessments, statement preparation and hearings?
- ☐ Are communication methods accessible, including clear language, written summaries and predictable scheduling?
- ☐ Has effective participation been reviewed throughout the proceedings, and not limited to hearings alone?

### Legal and Equality Duties

- ☐ Have duties under the Equality Act 2010, including reasonable adjustments and the Public Sector Equality Duty, been actively applied?

- ☐ Has Article 6 ECHR (effective participation and procedural fairness) been addressed within case management?

- ☐ Has Article 8 ECHR (respect for family life) been considered when assessing proportionality and outcomes?

### Assessments

- ☐ Has consideration been given to whether a specialist assessment is required rather than a generic parenting assessment?

- ☐ Has neurodivergence been identified early enough to inform the design and scope of any assessment?

- ☐ Does the assessment examine functioning with appropriate support and adjustments, rather than baseline presentation alone?

### Assessor Scrutiny

- ☐ What specialist neurodiversity training has the assessor completed?

- ☐ How recent and in-depth is that training?

- ☐ Who delivered the training and what are their credentials and expertise?
- ☐ Can the assessor demonstrate applied, practical expertise rather than solely theoretical awareness?

### Tools, Models and Toolkits

- ☐ Are the proposed assessment model and toolkit evidence-based and up to date?
- ☐ Are they relevant and appropriate to the family's specific needs?
- ☐ Do they support meaningful exploration of the asserted risks in the case?
- ☐ Are they delivered in a way the parent can understand, process and respond to effectively?

### Threshold and Risk Analysis

- ☐ Is threshold based on evidence of harm or risk, rather than neurodivergent traits?
- ☐ Are descriptors such as "non-compliant", "lacking insight" or "chaotic" supported by functional analysis?
- ☐ Has a clear distinction been drawn between difference and deficit?

### Trauma and Neurodivergence

- ☐ Has trauma been distinguished from neurodevelopmental need, recognising that the two may co-exist?
- ☐ Do expert instructions require consideration of both trauma and neurodivergence?
- ☐ Is there analysis of developmental history, masking and the persistence of behaviours over time?

### Children's Needs

- ☐ Has the child been screened or assessed for neurodivergence where indicated?
- ☐ Are the child's support needs addressed under section 17 of the Children Act 1989?
- ☐ Are placement, contact and care planning decisions informed by sensory, communication and regulation needs?

### Timetabling and Case Management

- ☐ Have assessments and adjustments been front-loaded to avoid narrative hardening?
- ☐ Has delay been avoided where it risks mischaracterising neurodivergent presentation as non-engagement or lack of insight?

☐ Is the care plan realistic, sustainable and workable in light of the parent's neurodivergent profile?

**Practitioner checklist: Spotting areas of challenge**

| **Area** | **Key question** | **Red flags** | **Grounds for challenge** |
|---|---|---|---|
| Identification | Was neurodivergence identified early? | No screening, reliance on stereotypes | Breach of s.17 Children Act 1989 / Equality Act 2010 |
| Assessment | Was an expert with dual expertise instructed? | Generic report, refusal of Part 25 assessment | *Re E* (2023) |
| Adjustments | Were reasonable adjustments provided? | Parent unable to follow hearings | Breach of FPR 3A / Art 6 ECHR |
| Contact | Was contact adapted to needs? | Child distressed in unsuitable environments | Breach of s.34 Children Act 1989 |
| Support | Were services provided under s.17? | Lack of EHCP, respite, or sensory support | Challenge adequacy of care plan |
| Trauma vs Neurodivergence | Did the expert distinguish causes? | Conflation of trauma with autism/ADHD | Unsafe assessment |
| Parenting Assessment | Was a specialist model used (e.g. MALD®)? | Reliance on generic social work tools | Breach of Equality Act / Art 8 ECHR |
| Participation | Were UCL-guided measures applied? | Parent confused or silenced | Breach of fair trial rights |

**Local authority compliance checklist**

| Duty | Action required | Evidence of compliance |
|---|---|---|
| Equality Act 2010 | Anticipate and make adjustments | Adjusted reports, communication logs |
| Children Act 1989, s.17 | Provide services for neurodivergent children | Child in Need plan, EHCP referrals |
| Children Act 1989, s.34 | Adapt contact arrangements | Records of sensory and communication adaptations |
| Human Rights Act 1998 (Arts 6, 8) | Ensure fair participation and proportionate intervention | Documented support services |
| Family Procedure Rules 2010, Part 3A | Secure participation directions | Court orders specifying adjustments |
| Trauma vs Neurodivergence | Commission experts able to distinguish both | Reports with developmental history |
| Parenting Assessments | Use appropriate specialist tool (e.g. MALD®) | Assessment reports citing model used |
| Incorporate UCL research | Apply UCL guidance in policy and training | Updated training records and policy documents |

## References

Department of Health (2000) *Framework for the Assessment of Children in Need and their Families.* London: The Stationery Office.

Family Justice Council (2025) *Guidance on Neurodiversity in the Family Justice System for Practitioners.* London: Judicial Office.

Felitti, V. J., Anda, R. F., Nordenberg, D., Williamson, D. F., Spitz, A. M., Edwards, V., Koss, M. P., & Marks, J. S. (1998) 'Relationship of Childhood Abuse and Household Dysfunction to Many of the Leading Causes of Death in Adults: The Adverse Childhood Experiences (ACE) Study', *American Journal of Preventive Medicine*, 14(4), pp. 245–258.

George, R., Crane, L. and Remington, A. (2020) *Autism and the Family Courts: A Grounded Study of Barriers and Experiences.* London: University College London.

McGaw, S., Scully, T. and Pritchard, J. (2010) *Parenting Assessment Manual Software (PAMS) User Guide.* University of Birmingham.

MALD (2024) *Model for Assessing Learning Difficulties and Vulnerabilities.* London: MALD Research Group.

Re C (A Child) [2011] EWCA Civ 521.

Re E (A Child) (Care and Placement Orders) [2023] EWCA Civ 721

# CHAPTER ELEVEN

# NEURODIVERGENCE IN PRIVATE LAW PROCEEDINGS

## Introduction

Domestic abuse remains one of the most complex and contested issues in private family law. Although there is now greater awareness, the intersection between domestic abuse and neurodivergence remains critically underdeveloped in both theory and practice. Private children law cases are often highly emotive and hinge on the court's assessment of credibility, capacity, and parenting insight. For neurodivergent parents and children, this environment can create profound challenges when their cognitive or behavioural differences are misunderstood.

This chapter examines how neurodivergence features in private children law proceedings, particularly where allegations of domestic abuse arise in contact disputes. In these contexts, neurodivergent traits can affect both how behaviour is interpreted and how evidence is assessed. The credibility-based nature of fact-finding hearings, combined with entrenched misconceptions about communication, affect, and behaviour, can disadvantage those whose presentation diverges from neurotypical expectations. By exploring the intersection of neurodivergence, domestic abuse, and evidential assessment, this chapter aims to help practitioners recognise and respond appropriately to the distinct risks and barriers faced by neurodivergent individuals in private children law proceedings. It concludes with a procedural roadmap and addresses the circumstances in which neurodivergence assessments may be adduced as expert evidence.

## The legal framework

Under the Children Act 1989, the welfare of the child is the court's paramount consideration (s.1(1)). Section 1(3) requires consideration of the child's physical, emotional, and educational needs, which encompass neurodevelopmental differences.

Allegations of domestic abuse frequently arise in private law proceedings. Practice Direction 12J and case law including *Re H-N and Others* [2021] EWCA Civ 448 and *Re K* [2022] EWCA Civ 463 provide guidance on how the court should approach such allegations and fact-finding hearings. These principles must be applied in a manner that accounts for neurodivergent presentation, communication styles, and participation needs, particularly where allegations of domestic abuse and credibility assessments intersect.

## Neurodivergence in the context of domestic abuse

To understand how domestic abuse dynamics may present in evidence, it is necessary to understand how neurodivergent coping strategies, particularly masking, develop.

When a neurodivergent person is repeatedly misunderstood, they begin to mask their true self to avoid rejection or conflict. This masking can lead to shame and self-blame causing them to become hypervigilant ensuring that their true self isn't revealed. This constant pressure of masking overwhelms the nervous system, increasing anxiety, burnout and creating a self-reinforcing loop of misunderstanding, self-suppression, and stress. This dynamic becomes particularly relevant when courts are looking at allegations of domestic abuse and when assessing credibility, parental capacity, and responses to abuse.

From childhood, many neurodivergent individuals are conditioned to mask their natural traits in order to gain social acceptance and safety. When such individuals later enter intimate relationships, their conditioning often translates into difficulty recognising coercive control or asserting boundaries. Within family proceedings, this may mean that a parent presents as compliant, confused, or emotionally flat, traits that can be easily misinterpreted as inconsistency or indifference. A partner's dismissive or controlling actions may be normalised because the neurodivergent individual has been taught to doubt their own perceptions. In cases of domestic abuse, the survivor may internalise blame or perceive the abuse as a consequence of "overreacting."

Perpetrators often exploit neurodivergent traits, such as honesty, literal interpretation, or social naivety, to manipulate and control (Brown et al., 2017). In court, these same traits can be weaponised to question credibility or parental capacity as will be shown later in this chapter. Over time, repeated invalidation and disbelief, both in personal relationships and during legal proceedings, produce hypervigilance, exhaustion, and trauma responses that affect behaviour and communication. These features are frequently invisible to the family courts but are crucial to understanding the presentation of neurodivergent parents in abusive relationships in proceedings.

## Features of neurodivergence increasing risk of abuse and affecting credibility in family proceedings

### Autism

Autistic individuals face distinct vulnerabilities to domestic abuse and coercive and controlling behaviour that intersect with evidential and procedural challenges in family law:

- People pleasing to "fit in" and complying without challenging to conform with social norms (Mogavero, 2016).

- Difficulty interpreting social cues or emotional subtext, which can obscure early warning signs of manipulation

- High levels of shame and self-blame that discourage disclosure or seeking help
- Social isolation due to sensory overwhelm and limited support networks
- Dependence on others for financial or practical support
- Co-occurring mental health conditions, such as anxiety or depression, that increase dependency

Perpetrators may exploit these vulnerabilities by reframing abuse as a "misunderstanding" or by blaming the autistic partner's "deficits". Within proceedings, such distortions can influence findings of fact or assessments of parenting. For instance, emotional withdrawal due to sensory overload might be misinterpreted as neglect. Literal communication may be presented as rudeness, evasiveness, being "difficult".

## ADHD

For individuals with ADHD, overlapping yet distinct risks emerge. Impulsivity, emotional intensity, and executive functioning challenges can be manipulated by abusers or misread by professionals. Common risk factors include:

- Difficulty regulating feelings which can be manipulated through patterns of idealisation and devaluation
- Difficulties with executive dysfunction which may be cited as evidence of irresponsibility, being lazy or lacking capacity to parent
- Low self-esteem stemming from years of internal and external criticism

- A heightened need for stimulation or novelty that can be manipulated through intermittent reinforcement.

In the courtroom, ADHD related difficulties can undermine perceived reliability. Inconsistency under stress or frustration during cross-examination may be mistaken for volatility, being aggressive, feeding narratives of instability or poor parental control.

## Misinterpretation of neurodivergent traits

Neurodivergent communication and regulation can be misread through a neurotypical lens. Common examples include:

| Neurodivergent Presentation | Common Misinterpretation | Reality |
|---|---|---|
| Flat affect or monotone speech | Coldness, lack of empathy | A self-regulatory response to stress |
| Limited eye contact | Dishonesty or evasiveness | A coping strategy for overstimulation |
| Overdetailed accounts | Manipulative or rehearsed | A grounding mechanism for recall |
| Variable memory | Fabrication | Impact of trauma, executive dysfunction and fear of saying the wrong thing |
| Shutdown or withdrawal | Passive aggression | Neurological overload or overwhelm |
| Literal responses | Argumentative | Direct processing style |

| Rapid or pressured speech (ADHD) | Volatility | Hyperarousal and anxiety |
|---|---|---|

These misreadings can profoundly distort truth-finding. A neurodivergent parent may appear detached or volatile, leading to unjust conclusions about credibility or parenting capacity.

Neurodivergent traits can be weaponised. Allegations of controlling behaviour, parental alienation, or unfitness may stem from misinterpreted coping mechanisms rather than intentional harm. Examples include:

- Autistic need for predictability reframed as controlling
- Adherence to routines portrayed as obsession
- Difficulty processing change misread as resistance
- Emotional dysregulation described as instability

The Family Justice Council Guidance (2025) cautions against using diagnostic labels as evidence of unsuitability or parental alienation. Assessors must distinguish between behaviour arising from neurodivergence and behaviour intended to manipulate.

### Neurodivergence and fact-finding hearings: credibility and demeanour

Fact-finding hearings frequently rely on assessments of credibility drawn from demeanour, consistency, and emotional presentation. Although these cues can often be treated as intuitive markers of truthfulness, they can be an unstable basis and unreliable when applied to neurodivergent individuals. When a court expects a witness to present in a narrow, conventional way, differences in communication style and regulation can be mistaken for indicators of deceit, manipulation, or lack of insight. The risk is not simply that the witness is misunderstood, but that the hearing process itself produces misleading "credibility signals" that then contaminate the court's evaluation of the underlying evidence.

Neurodivergent presentation may diverge from common assumptions about how a credible witness should look and sound. Limited eye contact, a monotone voice, unusual facial expression, reduced gesture, rigid posture, or appearing emotionally contained may be interpreted as coldness, indifference, or fabrication. Delayed responses, pauses, or apparently slow answering may be misread as evasiveness or an attempt to construct an answer. Differences in conversational timing, such as needing longer to start speaking or taking questions very literally, can be taken as non-cooperation. Overly detailed accounts, tangential answers, and difficulty summarising may be framed as rehearsed evidence, embellishment, or an attempt to overwhelm the court. In reality, these features commonly reflect functional differences in processing and communication, including the need for extra time to interpret questions, difficulty filtering and prioritising information under stress, heightened sensitivity to sensory input, and the use of self-regulation strategies to stay within a manageable window of arousal.

The courtroom environment magnifies these effects. Formality, unfamiliar routines, adversarial questioning, frequent interruptions, time pressure, and the expectation of rapid, concise responses create a setting that can push neurodivergent witnesses into cognitive overload. Under overload, speech may become disfluent, reasoning may appear rigid, and the witness may lose their ability to track the structure of the questioning. A witness may focus on accuracy at the expense of brevity, correcting small errors or returning repeatedly to contextual details because precision feels necessary to avoid being misunderstood. Where a witness has a history of masking or previous negative experiences with authority, they may default to highly controlled presentation, appearing calm or detached even while distressed. None of these behaviours reliably correlate with honesty. They correlate with coping.

Trauma can further compound these difficulties, particularly in cases involving domestic abuse, coercive control, or chronic fear. Trauma responses such as shutdown, dissociation, freezing, fawning, and hypervigilance can affect both presentation and recall. A traumatised witness may go blank, struggle to access detail on demand, or recall events in fragments rather than as a smooth, chronological narrative. They may remember sensory details but not dates, sequence, or timing, or they may recall some aspects vividly while other parts feel inaccessible. Apparent inconsistencies may reflect state-dependent memory, fear responses, or the way traumatic material is encoded and retrieved, rather than deliberate fabrication. If questioning becomes repetitive, confrontational, or fast paced, the witness may become increasingly dysregulated, less coherent, or more suggestible, creating exactly the kind of "inconsistency" that is later presented as proof of unreliability.

Practitioners must therefore be cautious not to equate emotional expressiveness with truthfulness. A neurodivergent survivor of abuse may present calmly, appear detached, smile inappropriately, or seem confused, not because allegations are fabricated, but because emotional suppression and cognitive overload can operate as protective responses. Conversely, distress, frustration, agitation, or dysregulation under cross-examination may be wrongly framed as aggression, instability, or lack of credibility, when it may instead reflect the witness reaching their limit of regulatory capacity. The same caution applies to perceived confidence. A witness who appears articulate and controlled is not necessarily more truthful than a witness who struggles, and a witness who is distressed is not necessarily exaggerating. The court's task is to test evidence, not to reward performance.

For practitioners, the key is to address these risks explicitly and early, rather than leaving the court to make unspoken inferences from presentation. Submissions should identify the specific features that may arise for the witness in question and explain, in functional terms, how those features relate to processing style and regulation. This is usually more effective than relying on diagnostic labels alone. The point is not that the witness should be treated as fragile, but that the conditions in which evidence is given should support accuracy and allow the court to test that evidence fairly. Adjustments should be presented as measures to preserve evidential reliability and procedural fairness, not as special treatment.

Participation directions, ground rules hearings, and adapted questioning can be central to this approach. These measures can reduce avoidable overload, support in understanding and produce clearer evidence. They can also reduce the likelihood that the witness's coping strategies are misread as credibility deficits. The court should be invited to focus on the content of the evidence, its external coherence with other material, and the plausibility of the account in context, rather than drawing conclusions from eye contact, tone, speed of recall, or the presence or absence of emotion. Where necessary, the court can be asked to record that demeanour is given limited weight, particularly where there are identified neurodivergent or trauma-related features that make demeanour a poor proxy for truthfulness.

Ultimately, a fair fact-finding process is not one in which every witness presents in the same way, but one in which every witness is enabled to give their best evidence.

## How perpetrators may exploit neurodivergent traits

These credibility risks are intensified where domestic abuse continues through the proceedings themselves. In private law cases, perpetrators may present as reasonable and solution-focused while using procedure and communication to exhaust, destabilise, and discredit the other parent. Neurodivergent individuals can be particularly vulnerable because sustained conflict, unpredictability, rapid decision-making, and confrontational communication can trigger overload, shutdown, or dysregulation. Those stress responses may then be presented as evidence that the neurodivergent parent is the problem.

Common tactics include repeated applications, threats of enforcement, tactical use of correspondence, and rigid or selective interpretation of orders. Perpetrators may escalate disputes around handovers, routines, and minor alleged breaches, knowing these are high pressure points where distress is most likely to show. They may create ambiguity, change arrangements at short notice, or insist on direct contact "for the child", then rely on the neurodivergent parent's difficulty with sudden change and confrontation to provoke a reaction. Neurodivergent parents may struggle to respond strategically in the moment and may appear disorganised, overly detailed, or reactive. Without a functional lens, this can be misread as hostility or non-compliance rather than as a predictable response to sustained provocation and stress.

Perpetrators may also attempt to weaponise neurodivergence within the narrative of the case. This can include selectively disclosing diagnoses, reframing coping strategies as controlling behaviour, portraying a need for structure or written communication as obstruction, or alleging parental alienation based on a child's distress or dysregulation. Professionals may misinterpret neurodivergent communication styles as manipulative or unstable, while the perpetrator's calm presentation is treated as credibility. The risk is that neurodivergent coping becomes pathologised and used to divert attention from coercive patterns.

Courts and professionals must distinguish coercive tactics from neurodivergent responses to stress, keeping the focus on patterns, context, and impact, including conduct within the proceedings. Practitioners can support this by naming the dynamics early, inviting scrutiny of the purpose and effect of repeated applications and handover disputes, and seeking case management and participation directions that reduce opportunities for provocation and misinterpretation.

## Neurodivergent children

A neurodivergent child may behave differently in each home due to sensory triggers, routines or relationship dynamics. Common scenarios can include:

- One parent insists the child is "fine" and claims behaviours only occur in the other parent's care. This may reflect environmental or sensory differences rather than fabrication
- A child may mask distress with one parent but experience meltdowns or shutdowns with the other, leading to accusations of influence
- A neurodivergent child may need shorter, structured contact or a safe, low-stimulation space to decompress
- Meltdowns after contact may reflect sensory overload from transitions, not a parent's inability to parent
- A preference for one environment may reflect predictability and regulation rather than "rejection" or alienation

Sensory and emotional regulation must be considered in cases involving neurodivergent children. A child's apparent rejection of a parent may reflect sensory discomfort rather than a parent exhibiting alienating behaviours.

Courts and professionals must examine the child's full relational context before making any recommendations or decisions. This means looking beyond isolated behaviours or diagnostic labels to understand the web of relationships that shape the child's daily experience. It involves exploring the child's attachments, patterns of communication, sensory profile, emotional regulation, and the quality of interactions with each caregiver. The latter should also include how adults respond to the child's needs, whether they can attune and adapt to the child's developmental and neurobiological profile.

### Procedural roadmap: where neurodivergence matters in private law proceedings

Neurodivergence can affect every stage of a private law case, not only the hearing itself. It matters from the first contact with the system because the process is cognitively and emotionally demanding, heavily dependent on written communication, and characterised by uncertainty. Early difficulties are often mislabelled as disengagement or lack of insight, when they may reflect processing load, executive functioning demands, or fear of being misunderstood.

### Issuing proceedings and safeguarding checks

At the point of issue and safeguarding checks, neurodivergent parties may struggle to complete forms concisely, organise chronology, or communicate in the expected style. They may disclose too much or too little, omit key context, or appear inconsistent as they recall information in fragments. Telephone-based safeguarding calls can be especially challenging where auditory processing differences or shutdown responses are present. If this stage produces a partial or distorted picture, it can set the tone for later professional interpretation and influence early risk framing.

When statements and position documents are prepared, the ability to summarise, prioritise, and maintain a coherent narrative becomes central. Neurodivergent parties may be accurate but non-linear, may write with intense detail, or may struggle to identify what the court will treat as relevant. They may also find it difficult to respond to allegations point by point under time pressure, particularly where the other party's case is sprawling or rhetorically framed. This is a stage where functional explanation and careful drafting can prevent a neurodivergent communication style being treated as a credibility defect.

### Interim hearings

Interim hearings and directions appointments place particular pressure on processing speed and comprehension. Neurodivergent parties may struggle to follow rapid exchanges, shifting proposals, and judicial indications delivered orally in a short hearing. They may agree to arrangements they do not understand, not because they consent, but because they are overloaded and trying to end the interaction. Clear written orders, time to process proposals, and structured communication about next steps can be decisive for fairness and compliance.

### Fact-finding hearing

If a fact-finding hearing is listed, neurodivergence matters not only to witness evidence but to case management. The way questions are framed, the pace of cross-examination, the handling of documents, and the interpretation of demeanour can all affect the quality of evidence and the risk of misinterpretation. Similarly, where section 7 work or other assessments are directed, neurodivergent presentation may affect professional interviews and the interpretation of parenting capacity, particularly if assessors equate regulation difficulties under stress with baseline incapacity.

### DRA/final hearing

At dispute resolution and final hearing stages, neurodivergent needs often reappear as difficulties negotiating under pressure, responding to new proposals, or understanding the practical implications of arrangements. Orders that rely on flexibility, informal agreement, or constant renegotiation can be susceptible to breakdown and conflict. A procedural roadmap that anticipates these points allows practitioners to seek adaptations early, reduce avoidable stress, and support the court to obtain clearer evidence and make more durable welfare-based decisions.

## Disclosure of assessments into proceedings

If a party seeks to adduce a copy of their neurodivergence assessment into proceedings, it should be treated as expert evidence and a formal application for permission must be made in accordance with FPR Part 25. In family proceedings, a party may not put expert evidence before the court without permission, and the court will only grant permission where the expert evidence is necessary to assist the court to resolve the proceedings.

That remains the position even where the assessment was obtained privately and before proceedings began. Practice Direction 25A makes clear that permission is required to put any expert evidence before the court, including expert evidence obtained pre-proceedings, and in children proceedings evidence resulting from expert instruction or assessment without the required permission is inadmissible unless the court rules otherwise.

The application should be made as soon as possible and in private law proceedings no later than the First Hearing Dispute Resolution Appointment unless the court directs otherwise. Any application made must be compliant with FPR Part 25.

## Practical checklist for practitioners

### Early identification and framing

- ☐ Ask at the earliest stage whether any party/child is neurodivergent (diagnosed or suspected) and identify functional impacts (processing speed, sensory sensitivities, communication style, executive functioning, regulation under stress).

- ☐ Record needs in a neutral, functional way (avoid "label = risk" thinking).
- ☐ Consider whether domestic abuse dynamics may be interacting with masking, shutdown, fawning, hypervigilance, or overload.

**Participation and fairness (throughout)**

- ☐ Consider participation directions and/or a ground rules hearing early (not the week before evidence).
- ☐ Seek adjustments that improve evidential reliability (not "special treatment"), for example simplified, short questions (one point at a time), additional time to process and answer, regular breaks/shorter sessions, permission to have questions in writing in advance (where appropriate), remote attendance/screen breaks/reduced sensory load (lighting, noise, positioning), and agreement on how interruptions will be managed.
- ☐ Ensure orders and directions are clear, written, and unambiguous; avoid "reasonable flexibility" language that creates conflict.

**Safeguarding and first hearings**

- ☐ Support the party to present a clear chronology (even if short) and identify key incidents, patterns, and impact.

- ☐ Anticipate difficulties with forms/conciseness; assist in prioritising relevance and explaining why detail may be coping rather than evasion.
- ☐ Flag any telephone-based safeguarding barriers (auditory processing, anxiety, shutdown) and request suitable alternatives where needed.

**Statements and evidence preparation**

- ☐ Structure statements tightly (headings, dates, issues) and keep a separate "detail annex" if necessary.
- ☐ Explain potential presentation features in functional terms (e.g., flat affect, limited eye contact, pauses, over-detail, variable recall).
- ☐ Where trauma is relevant, link memory/consistency issues to trauma responses and stress physiology without over-pathologising.

**Fact-finding hearings**

- ☐ Invite the court to place limited weight on demeanour where neurodivergent/trauma features are identified.
- ☐ Ensure questioning style is adapted: slower pace, fewer compound questions, explicit time references, and avoidance of sarcasm or implication-based questioning.
- ☐ Plan document handling (bundles, tabs, page references) to reduce overload and consider "document-free" questioning where feasible.

- ☐ Monitor signs of overload/shutdown and be ready to seek a break or adjustment in real-time.

### Domestic abuse and litigation abuse

- ☐ Consider whether coercive control is continuing through proceedings (repeat applications, tactical correspondence, handover disputes).
- ☐ Keep focus on patterns, context, purpose and impact, not isolated incidents or "presentation".
- ☐ Where provocation is likely, seek case management to reduce contact points and ambiguity (structured handovers, written-only channels, fixed routines).

### Neurodivergent children

- ☐ Analyse behaviour across both households through a sensory/regulation lens (transitions, environment, routines, attunement).
- ☐ Guard against mislabelling masking/meltdowns as "alienation" without relational and sensory assessment.
- ☐ Ensure contact proposals are realistic for the child's regulation needs (predictability, decompression time, low stimulation, gradual change).

**Experts and assessments**

- ☐ Treat neurodivergence assessments as expert evidence and consider permission requirements and necessity.

- ☐ If relying on an assessment, make an early, compliant application and explain how it assists the court (participation, evidence reliability, welfare analysis).

- ☐ Ensure the court and professionals use the assessment to understand function and support needs, not as a proxy for risk or parenting capacity.

**Professional reports and welfare analysis**

- ☐ Challenge reports that equate dysregulation under stress with baseline incapacity.

- ☐ Ask assessors to distinguish neurodivergent traits from coercive, manipulative, or controlling behaviour.

- ☐ Ensure recommendations are workable and reduce conflict triggers (clarity, routine, predictability, limited renegotiation).

**Final orders**

- ☐ Draft orders with specificity (times, locations, contingencies, communication method).

- ☐ Build in predictable review points rather than open-ended "flexibility".

☐ Consider a communication framework that reduces overload and dispute (structured written format, response times, single platform)

**References**

Brown, A., Smith, R. and Jones, T. (2017) *Coercive control and cognitive difference: Understanding the exploitation of neurodivergent traits in intimate partner abuse. Journal of Interpersonal Violence*, 32(15), pp. 2254–2273.

Chapman, E. (2023) *The invisible abuse: Coercive control and neurodivergence in family law contexts. Family Law Review*, 12(3), pp. 145–162.

Family Justice Council (2025) *Guidance on Neurodiversity and Family Proceedings.* London: Judicial College.

Hollomotz, A. (2013) *Disability, abuse and social policy: Understanding vulnerability and protection.* Bristol: Policy Press.

Mogavero, M.C. (2016) 'Autistic women and intimate partner violence: A review of the literature and implications for practice.' *Journal of Family Violence*, 31(8), pp. 1121–1130.

Peters, L. (2023) *The Neurodivergence Trauma Cycle: Invalidation, masking and chronic distress.* London: Routledge.

Re H-N and Others (Children) (Domestic Abuse: Findings of Fact Hearings) [2021] EWCA Civ 448.

The Children Act 1989 (UK).

The Equality Act 2010 (UK).

European Convention on Human Rights (1950), Article 6.

# MORE BOOKS BY
# LAW BRIEF PUBLISHING

A selection of our other titles available now:-

- 'A Practical Guide to Probation Breaches and Other Applications' by Mark Thomas
- 'A Practical Guide to Remarriage and Divorce' by Cordelia Williams & Claire Howard
- 'A Practical Guide to Privacy, Transparency, Reporting Restrictions and Closed Proceedings in the Court of Protection' by Laura Mannering
- 'Beaumont on Barristers – A Guide to Defending Disciplinary Proceedings (Second Edition)' by Marc Beaumont
- 'A Practical Guide to Payments for Environmental Services' by Ben Sharples
- 'A Practical Guide to the Law of Pregnancy and Maternity at Work' by Rebecca Thomas
- 'A Practical Guide to Redundancy – Second Edition' by Philip Hyland & Collette Moore
- 'A Practical Guide to International Issues for Scottish Family Lawyers' by Susie Mountain, Donna McKay, Ken MacDonald
- 'A Practical Guide to the Law on Deprivation of Liberty' by Ben Troke
- 'A Practical Guide to Rights over Airspace and Subsoil – Second Edition' by Daniel Gatty
- 'A Practical Guide to the Law in Relation to Inquests' by Ramya Nagesh
- 'A Practical Guide to the Construction and Rectification of Wills and Trust Instruments (Second Edition)' by Edward Hewitt
- 'A Practical Guide to Data Protection in Social Housing' by Clare Paterson
- 'A Practical Guide to Spousal Maintenance – Second Edition' by Liz Cowell
- 'A Practical Guide to International Parental Child Abduction Law (England and Wales)' by Dr Onyója Momoh
- 'A Practical Guide to Deprivation of British Citizenship' by Sean Ell
- 'A Practical Guide to Commercial Property Service Charges' by Rachel Garton
- 'A Practical Guide to Clinical Negligence – Third Edition' by Geoffrey Simpson-Scott (Geoff)
- 'A Practical Guide to the Rights of Grandparents in Children Proceedings – Second Edition' by Stuart Barlow

| |
|---|
| 'The Electronic Communications Code: A Practical Guide – Second Edition' by Kerry Bretherton KC, James Castle, Mark Loveday |
| 'A Practical Guide to the Independent School Standards – September 2023 Edition' by Sarah McKimm |
| 'A Practical Guide to Estate Administration and Crypto Assets' by Richard Marshall |
| 'A Practical Guide to Parental Alienation in Private and Public Law Children Cases' by Sam King QC & Frankie Shama |
| 'Contested Heritage – Removing Art from Land and Historic Buildings' by Richard Harwood QC, Catherine Dobson, David Sawtell |
| 'The Limits of Separate Legal Personality: When Those Running a Company Can Be Held Personally Liable for Losses Caused to Third Parties Outside of the Company' by Dr Mike Wilkinson |
| 'A Practical Guide to Transgender Law' by Robin Moira White & Nicola Newbegin |
| 'A Practical Guide to 'Stranded Spouses' in Family Law' by Mani Singh Basi |
| 'A Practical Guide to Residential Freehold Conveyancing' by Lorraine Richardson |
| 'A Practical Guide to Pensions on Divorce for Lawyers' by Bryan Scant |
| 'A Practical Guide to Challenging Sham Marriage Allegations in Immigration Law' by Priya Solanki |
| 'A Practical Guide to Digital Communications Evidence in Criminal Law' by Sam Willis |
| 'A Practical Guide to Legal Rights in Scotland' by Sarah-Jane Macdonald |
| 'A Practical Guide to New Build Conveyancing' by Paul Sams & Rebecca East |
| 'A Practical Guide to Inherited Wealth on Divorce' by Hayley Trim |
| 'A Practical Guide to Practice Direction 12J and Domestic Abuse in Private Law Children Proceedings' by Rebecca Cross & Malvika Jaganmohan |
| 'A Practical Guide to Confiscation and Restraint' by Narita Bahra QC, John Carl Townsend, David Winch |
| 'A Practical Guide to the Law of Forests in Scotland' by Philip Buchan |
| 'A Practical Guide to Health and Medical Cases in Immigration Law' by Rebecca Chapman & Miranda Butler |
| 'A Practical Guide to Bad Character Evidence for Criminal Practitioners by Aparna Rao |
| 'A Practical Guide to Extradition Law post-Brexit' by Myles Grandison et al |
| 'A Practical Guide to Hoarding and Mental Health for Housing Lawyers' by Rachel Coyle |

‘Stephens on Contractual Indemnities’ by Richard Stephens

‘A Practical Guide to the EU Succession Regulation’ by Richard Frimston

‘A Practical Guide to Solicitor and Client Costs – Second Edition’ by Robin Dunne

‘Constructive Dismissal – Practice Pointers and Principles’ by Benjimin Burgher

‘A Practical Guide to Religion and Belief Discrimination Claims in the Workplace’ by Kashif Ali

‘A Practical Guide to the Law of Medical Treatment Decisions’ by Ben Troke

‘Fundamental Dishonesty and QOCS in Personal Injury Proceedings: Law and Practice’ by Jake Rowley

‘A Practical Guide to the Law in Relation to School Exclusions’ by Charlotte Hadfield & Alice de Coverley

‘A Practical Guide to Divorce for the Silver Separators’ by Karin Walker

‘The Right to be Forgotten – The Law and Practical Issues’ by Melissa Stock

‘A Practical Guide to Planning Law and Rights of Way in National Parks, the Broads and AONBs’ by James Maurici QC, James Neill et al

‘A Practical Guide to Election Law’ by Tom Tabori

‘A Practical Guide to the Law in Relation to Surrogacy’ by Andrew Powell

‘A Practical Guide to Claims Arising from Fatal Accidents – Second Edition’ by James Patience

‘A Practical Guide to Asbestos Claims’ by Jonathan Owen & Gareth McAloon

‘A Practical Guide to Stamp Duty Land Tax in England and Northern Ireland’ by Suzanne O’Hara

‘A Practical Guide to the Law of Farming Partnerships’ by Philip Whitcomb

‘A Practical Guide to the Law of Unlawful Eviction and Harassment – Second Edition’ by Stephanie Lovegrove

‘A Practical Guide to Costs in Personal Injury Claims – Second Edition’ by Matthew Hoe

‘A Practical Guide to the General Data Protection Regulation (GDPR) – Second Edition’ by Keith Markham

‘A Practical Guide to Working with Litigants in Person and McKenzie Friends in Family Cases’ by Stuart Barlow

‘Protecting Unregistered Brands: A Practical Guide to the Law of Passing Off’ by Lorna Brazell

‘A Practical Guide to Secondary Liability and Joint Enterprise Post-Jogee’ by Joanne Cecil & James Mehigan

'A Practical Guide to the Pre-Action RTA Claims Protocol for Personal Injury Lawyers' by Antonia Ford

'A Practical Guide to Neighbour Disputes and the Law' by Alexander Walsh

'A Practical Guide to Coercive Control for Legal Practitioners and Victims' by Rachel Horman

'A Practical Guide to the Law of Driverless Cars – Second Edition'

by Alex Glassbrook, Emma Northey & Scarlett Milligan

'A Practical Guide to TOLATA Claims' by Greg Williams

'A Practical Guide to Elderly Law – Second Edition' by Justin Patten

'A Practical Guide to Responding to Housing Disrepair and Unfitness Claims' by Iain Wightwick

'A Practical Guide to the Law of Bullying and Harassment in the Workplace' by Philip Hyland

'How to Be a Freelance Solicitor: A Practical Guide to the SRA-Regulated Freelance Solicitor Model' by Paul Bennett

'A Practical Guide to Prison Injury Claims' by Malcolm Johnson

'A Practical Guide to Advising Clients at the Police Station' by Colin Stephen McKeown-Beaumont

'A Practical Guide to Antisocial Behaviour Injunctions – Second Edition' by Iain Wightwick

'Practical Mediation: A Guide for Mediators, Advocates, Advisers, Lawyers, and Students in Civil, Commercial, Business, Property, Workplace, and Employment Cases' by Jonathan Dingle with John Sephton

'The Mini-Pupillage Workbook' by David Boyle

'A Practical Guide to Crofting Law' by Brian Inkster

'A Practical Guide to the Law of Domain Names and Cybersquatting' by Andrew Clemson

'A Practical Guide to the Law of Gender Pay Gap Reporting' by Harini Iyengar

'NHS Whistleblowing and the Law' by Joseph England

'Employment Law and the Gig Economy' by Nigel Mackay & Annie Powell

'A Practical Guide to Noise Induced Hearing Loss (NIHL) Claims' by Andrew Mckie, Ian Skeate, Gareth McAloon

'An Introduction to Beauty Negligence Claims – A Practical Guide for the Personal Injury Practitioner' by Greg Almond

'Intercompany Agreements for Transfer Pricing Compliance' by Paul Sutton

'Zen and the Art of Mediation' by Martin Plowman

'A Practical Guide to Adoption for Family Lawyers' by Graham Pegg

| |
|---|
| 'A Practical Guide to Industrial Disease Claims' by Andrew Mckie & Ian Skeate |
| 'A Practical Guide to Conducting a Sheriff Court Proof' by Andrew Stevenson |
| 'A Practical Guide to Vicarious Liability' by Mariel Irvine |
| 'A Practical Guide to Applications for Landlord's Consent and Variation of Leases' by Mark Shelton |
| 'A Practical Guide to Relief from Sanctions Post-Mitchell and Denton' by Peter Causton |
| 'A Practical Guide to Equity Release for Advisors' by Paul Sams |
| 'A Practical Guide to Financial Services Claims' by Chris Hegarty |
| 'A Practical Guide to Financial Ombudsman Service Claims' by Adam Temple & Robert Scrivenor |
| 'A Practical Guide to Running Housing Disrepair and Cavity Wall Claims – Second Edition' by Andrew Mckie & Ian Skeate |
| 'A Practical Guide to Holiday Sickness Claims – Second Edition' by Andrew Mckie & Ian Skeate |
| 'Arguments and Tactics for Personal Injury and Clinical Negligence Claims' by Dorian Williams |
| 'A Practical Guide to Drone Law' by Rufus Ballaster, Andrew Firman, Eleanor Clot |
| 'On Experts: CPR35 for Lawyers and Experts' by David Boyle |
| 'An Introduction to Personal Injury Law' by David Boyle |

These books and more are available to order online direct from the publisher at www.lawbriefpublishing.com, where you can also read free sample chapters. For any queries, call us on 0844 587 2383 or email us at mail@lawbriefpublishing.com.

Our books are all generally in stock at www.amazon.co.uk with free next day delivery for Prime members, and at good legal bookshops such as Wildy & Sons.

We are regularly launching new books in our series of practical day-to-day practitioners' guides. Visit our website and join our free newsletter to be kept informed and to receive special offers, free chapters, etc.

You can also follow us on Twitter at www.twitter.com/lawbriefpub.

www.ingramcontent.com/pod-product-compliance
Lightning Source LLC
LaVergne TN
LVHW022047200926
848481LV00003B/816